EUROPAN 16
AUSTRIA

LIVING
CITIES

CONTENTS

5   Editorial, Introduction

12   **LIVING CITIES**
13   **Andreas Hofer**
      The Right to Space
17   **Elke Krasny**
      Care
19   **Elisabeth Merk**
      Theses for a Viable City
23   **Bart Lootsma**
      If You Want to Look Back, Then to Modernism
27   **Paola Viganò**
      Design the Transition: A Few Notes on an Emerging Culture
31   **Bas Princen**
      The Room of Peace (Siena)

34   **GRAZ**
      Trading the Big and the Small
39   **Akil Scafe-Smith**
      Opening Gruen's Box: Civic Prospects in Graz
44   Projects

64   **KLAGENFURT**
      Educating Inclusivity
69   **Benni Eder**
      Where Will All the Buses Go?
74   Projects

88   **LINZ**
      Expansion from Within
95   **Susanne Eliasson**
      Prototypes That Tell a Story
98   Projects

106   Jury
110   Teams
112   Timeline

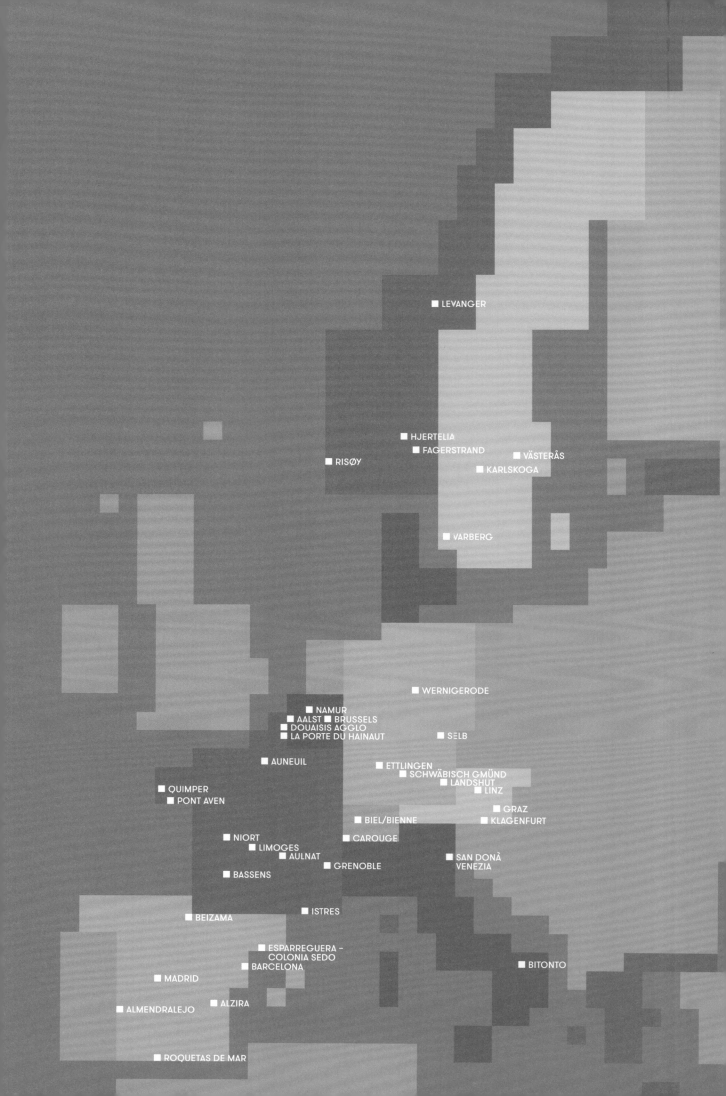

EDITORIAL

Iris Kaltenegger

Who wouldn't understand that breaking the news to the awarded teams is one of the highlights in every EUROPAN round? After lengthy analyses and discussions in jury sessions, the site partners and we from EUROPAN Austria are, by that time, already so familiar with the projects that we can hardly wait to learn about the young, spirited mind(s) behind them.

In the catalogue section of this publication, the winning proposals on the three Austrian sites of Graz, Klagenfurt, and Linz are presented along with statements from the jury and personal remarks from the authors, allowing a glimpse behind the scenes. For Michalis Ntourakos, the Linz site winner, EUROPAN 16 marks the closing of a personal ten-year cycle dedicated to international architecture competitions for 'young' planners: 'What a fine way to "end" this trajectory (#almost40) of five consecutive EUROPAN sessions, among many other competitions.' Free Mühlgang, the runner-up team in Graz, met at the Architecture School of Madrid: 'After years of wandering across the world, EUROPAN 16 gave us the chance to reconnect and materialise the dreams, ideals, programmes, and concepts we pursue.' They are currently based in Madrid and Los Angeles. In total, the 168 participants on the three Austrian sites originate from 24 different countries. This and more statistical data are spread throughout the book and well visualised by the graphic designers, sensomatic. They show the power of EUROPAN to bring people together from all over the world in a collective effort to improve our environment.

The EUROPAN 16 topic 'Living Cities' takes up the challenge to profoundly question and rethink our ideas on how we want to live together in the future. How can a balanced, inclusive, and socially just way of life manifest itself in our living environment? A theme so vast and essentially powerful is hard to grasp. Thus, the moment you find the partners who understand the importance of this endeavour, who have the instruments to ground it and the confidence to do this with a new generation of planners, is another significant highlight in the whole process. I am still impressed by the rather unconventional openness of Martin Poppmeier, the developer and site owner in Graz: 'There should be no limits to the design – the ideas must come from you!', he declares with an expecting and smiling face in the info-clip. Who wouldn't be intrigued by that? And indeed, the invitation in Graz was followed by big ideas and high visionary power.

This is the beauty and the strength of the EUROPAN competition: It provides a safe space to think and to critically question well-worn paths. EUROPAN is a concrete chance to pause, re-think, and set off for real change. The theme 'Living Cities' is not only about good urban values and well composed spaces, it is far more about revealing the fertile ground of future living conditions embedded in a metabolic reading. When we talk about living cities '[...] the demand for participation remains, for a space that is accessible to everyone, everywhere', declares Andreas Hofer in his article 'The Right to Space'. You will find many more inspiring and thought-provoking arguments elaborated by selected thinkers, like the ten theses for a viable city discussed by Elisabeth Merk, in the topic section of this catalogue.

They are illustrated with the photographs by Bas Princen, shown at the 14th Venice Architecture Biennale 2014. His installation of Lorenzetti's frescos painted in the Sala dei Nove in Siena on 'good and bad governance' are a mute reminder of what is at stake. The future of our cities will be decided within the next decade. In the transition process towards a life-sustaining environment, planning will play a crucial role, but only if it is prepared to make new alliances and to embrace all concerns of human and non-human agents.

As always, this EUROPAN competition, with all its ambitiously involved actors, is a catalyser and a step towards a positive outcome.

Dear reader, immerse yourself in this interesting topic full of powerful directions and spirited possibilities. For me, this publication is definitely yet another highlight!

Iris Kaltenegger is an architect and general secretary of EURO-PAN Austria. She is the founder and president of Open House Vienna and teaches at the Technical University of Vienna.

INTRODUCTION

Bernd Vlay

Welcome to a new adventure! BUT: What the hell does metabolism do? The challenge to introduce this exciting publication has animated me to begin my text with an exclamation, followed by a question. Both are connected by a 'BUT' which hints at a delicate specificity:
This is the catalogue about the EUROPAN 16 results of the three Austrian sites of Graz, Linz, and Klagenfurt. Together with 40 sites from nine countries, they were participating in the 16th round of EUROPAN. Its theme, *Living Cities*, has underlined EUROPAN's role as a design laboratory that claims the indispensability of our planning culture when it comes to repairing the future of our cities and territories.
Living Cities – Metabolic and Inclusive Vitalities provided a fertile ground for inviting the young generation of architects, urban planners, urban designers, and landscape architects to make a point: to pick one or more sites as a test field to challenge the young generation's expertise: how to breathe *metabolic* and *inclusive* vitalities into them, tackling, on the one hand, their social, economic, ecological, and cultural 'misbehaviours', as well as exploring, on the other hand, new opportunities due to ongoing or upcoming transformations (new infrastructures, development dynamics).

Now, what is the delicate specificity I was mentioning? Without exception, all the winning teams of the Austrian sites come from abroad! This is great, as it is EUROPAN's ambition to cross nations. Yet, it is also symptomatic. Not only in Austria but all over Europe we face a striking absence of Austrian winning teams diagnosing their unfamiliarity as for the *Living Cities'* impact on methods and ways of designing. The documentation of the winning projects in this catalogue, as well as the reflections of the international jury members (by the way again, all from abroad), might contribute to curing this unfamiliarity. Their thoughtful translations of the *Living Cities'* empathetic concerns into urban, architectural, and landscape projects point to a new awareness of responsibilities, embedding the concrete competition task in a larger, multiscale process of transformation that unveils and creates surprising values for the site. We can observe a concern for building new relations and relationships between things, actions, and processes which not only envision a promising horizon for the sites themselves but, among some of the projects, imagine a new horizon for the city and the territory, questioning its actual modus operandi. Multi-layered strategies construct material and processual relations across multiple scales, ostensively answering the question which many young Austrian architects symptomatically might have asked themselves: 'What the hell does metabolism do?'

Andreas Hofer's passionate plea for a *Living City* urges us to secure the 'Right to Space' by rethinking the relationship between city and countryside, implying that the 'inner city must reinvent itself'. As all three Austrian sites are located in the inner city, I will conduct a short tour through the winning projects to find out in what way their multi-layered agenda might contribute to the *Living City*'s exigency of reinventing the inner city.

The travelogue of my tour is a series of micro-episodes based on provocative falsifications. They refer to the inspiring effects of René Magritte's *The Treachery of Images* ('Ceci n'est pas une pipe'), somehow flashlighting a special concern which all winning projects seem to share: to uncover the new behind the curtains of the already there.

INTRODUCTION

GRAZ I FREE MÜHLGANG
Water Is Not Water – Discovering New Opportunities in the Already There
To 'build new relationships with the geography of a place and its landscapes' (Paola Viganò) can turn a transitional threshold into a place in its own right, as 'Free Mühlgang' impressively demonstrates. Water becomes the element of imaginary opportunities, for public space as well as for the programming of the building(s).

GRAZ I POST-SHOPPING
A Mall Is Not a Mall – Re-enacting the Mall as Public Space
Akil Scafe Smith's contribution in this publication ends with a provocative remark about 'another' vision of the shopping mall relating to the mall's forgotten mission as it was imagined by its homesick founder, the Austrian architect Victor Gruen. Gruen longed for repairing California's suburban desert by enriching the necessity of shopping with the added value of a liveable public realm, memorising the lost heritage of the European city. 'Post-Shopping' demonstrates the urgent need for a new mission of the mall rediscovering its culture as a caretaker of public space.

GRAZ I URBAN SOLUTIONS SUPERSTRUCTURE
Supply Is Not Supply – Provoking a New Awareness of Resources
For centuries, we have been used to making deals to our advantages. Delegation and outsourcing have become our tools of comfort, instrumentalising the out-there as a resource to be harvested. Our cities, as well, have been participating in this global deal. The appearance of the superstructures in Graz is an intriguing return of the suppressed. Their provocative and at the same time seductive presence relentlessly creates awareness about the symptomatic denial of proactively spatialising circular processes.

KLAGENFURT | 5 SQUARES
5 Squares Are Not 5 Squares – Exploring a New Culture of Mobility
The winning team's 5 squares identify a new realm of public space, driven by the transformative capacity of a new paradigm of mobility: The 5 squares are absorbed within a ring-like, slow-motion environment deviating as an inclusive public *parcour* through Klagenfurt's inner city, which re-performs itself through a different culture of (non)speed and connectivity (intermodality).

KLAGENFURT I TRACING DOMAINS
A Use Is Not a Use – Creating Proactive Inclusion in Public Space
The project's 'laboratory for domestic prototypes' compiles the existing spectrum of dispersed uses, cross-programming them into seducing places which proactively suggest new synergies between uses, establishing vital relationships, blending learning and doing, consuming and producing, walking and enjoying – the way how uses are spatialised and allowed to act makes them powerful agents for an inclusive public space.

LINZ
A House Is Not a House
Elke Krasny's remarks on care remind us of the planetary scale of the object – a local 'thing' with global responsibilities. No matter how small architectural interventions might be – they always matter for the sake of the planet. 'Bio-based Idiolect' demonstrates how a renovation of existing residential buildings can reconfigure the culture of living, negotiate climate change, save resources, and trigger an inclusive milieu for the Froschberg district in Linz.

During my tour through the projects, I was able to learn that the creation of living cities is based on the mission to re-discover. There is nothing useful about newness in itself. Instead, the projects claim a 'coup of resources': to repair the future of the past by excavating values that were lost, suppressed, or cancelled out, as beautifully described in Bart Lootsma's memories of his post-war housing childhood, which excavate the carefully designed ecologies behind the curtain of the disgraced modernist realm of Amsterdam – another living city.

Facing Bart Lootsma's re-discovery of a lost 'milieu', I would like to end my introduction with an appeal that amplifies Elisabeth Merk's concern 'not [to] eliminate disparities between rural and urban areas, but rather reinforce the respective qualities through intelligent cooperation': Let us not eliminate the potential of the 'already there' but rather re-perform its latent qualities through careful, imperturbable, and fundamental exploration. Raise the curtain for *Living Cities*!

Bernd Vlay is the president of EUROPAN Austria, a member of the scientific committee of EUROPAN Europe and was a member of the international jury for EUROPAN 16. He is an architect, urbanist and researcher, director of Studio VlayStreeruwitz and teacher at the Academy of Fine Arts in Vienna.

ENTRIES PER SITE

40 SITES IN 9 COUNTRIES

- **SCHWÄBISCH GMÜND,** GERMANY: 10
- **CAROUGE,** SWITZERLAND: 10
- **BARCELONA,** SPAIN: 11
- **BITONTO,** ITALY: 11
- **DOUAISIS AGGLO,** FRANCE: 11
- **NAMUR,** BELGIUM: 11
- **ALZIRA,** SPAIN: 12
- **ALMENDRALEJO,** SPAIN: 12
- **SELB,** GERMANY: 12
- **BASSENS/BORDEAUX MÉTROPOLE,** FRANCE: 13
- **ESPARREGUERA COLONIAL SEDÓ,** SPAIN: 13
- **GRAZ,** AUSTRIA: 13
- **LINZ,** AUSTRIA: 13
- **KARLSKOGA,** SWEDEN: 13
- **SAN DONÀ VENEZIA,** ITALY: 13
- **VÄSTERÅS,** SWEDEN: 14
- **ISTRES,** FRANCE: 15
- **LA PORTE DU HAINAUT,** FRANCE: 15
- **AULNAT,** FRANCE: 15

AALST, BELGIUM: 16

BIEL/BIENNE, SWITZERLAND: 16

BRUSSELS CAPITAL REGION, BELGIUM: 16

GRENOBLE, FRANCE: 16

QUIMPER, FRANCE: 16

ETTLINGEN, FRANCE: 17

VARBERG, SWEDEN: 18

LANDSHUT, GERMANY: 19

KLAGENFURT, AUSTRIA: 20

AUNEUIL, FRANCE: 20

LIMOGES, FRANCE: 22

FAGERSTRAND, NORWAY: 22

RISØY, NORWAY: 22

WERNIGERODE, GERMANY: 25

ROQUETAS DE MAR, SPAIN: 25

LEVANGER, NORWAY: 26

PONT AVEN, FRANCE: 27

HJERTELIA, NORWAY: 30

BEIZAMA, SPAIN: 37

LIVING
CITIES

THE RIGHT TO SPACE

LIVING CITIES

Andreas Hofer

Industrialisation hit the landscape like a bomb. What had previously been a cramped, five-minute city splintered in space. Once the city walls were razed, the city spilled out into the surrounding area. Gold prospector camps grew into short-lived towns and industrial areas into urban regions. When the dust settled, the gravitational forces of capitalism formed rings, as with Saturn, but here rings of difference and specialisation. The Chicago School of Sociology described this in the nineteen-twenties. Of course, there had always been castles and palaces but never a comprehensive social allocation of space. Everything had its specialised place, did not disturb each another and degenerated into monofunctional boredom. Political housing systems, contradicting subsidies, a policy that seems to be dictated directly by construction company headquarters and which, with the watering can at the end, has a pot ready for anyone willing to build, as well as dreams of single-family houses cemented the social and functional wasteland. And now we are faced with the dubious and futureless result of 150 years of Fordist specialisation and the question of its reprogramming.

The centres specialising in shopping and culture lose their function, the suburbs of the affluent had always been boring and remain so, the adjoining middle-class districts, rutted by transportation infrastructures, fight for identity, then utilitarian commercial areas that are separated by industrially cleared agriculture form a metropolitan patchwork and the periphery left behind on the other side; many like to call it countryside.

Amazing how difficult this figure is to grasp. The older modernists optimised individual aspects in their intellectual silos and believed that their prototypes would become the city of the future. In recent decades, the critical generations of architects negotiated the city as a contested terrain within a narrow radius — in many cases from their own experience of their detested origins in the suburbs. It is only recently that they have taken on the city in-between, the agglomeration, in which they used to build at best their complicated first works — mostly single-family houses — for their relatives. Everyone is talking about the urban century and a majority of people who live in cities. But in fact, suburbanisation won, pushing out the fringes in which much of the rural is lost and little of the urban is gained.

The inner city must reinvent itself, since it no longer functions as a location of high prices, as a centre of purchasing power. The agglomerated fringes can be transformed into districts that are the local world for the majority of the population and the countryside is, just as ETH Basel claimed in its 2005 publication *Die Schweiz. Ein städtebauliches Porträt*, a resort for city dwellers looking for relaxation and a retreat for nature-loving freaks, perhaps meanwhile also for inner city-weary dropouts with broadband connection who have been driven away by insane speculation.

When we talk about living cities, we mean these complex structures, certainly no longer the squatting in the centre, the fixation on a long-lost battle for the city. At the same time, however, the demand for participation remains, for a space that is accessible to everyone, everywhere. If we give up this demand, we will capitulate to the laws of the market and accept a social segregation that is arguably the core of many social divisions we are currently experiencing. Democracy is only possible when society in all its facets can be everywhere.

LIVING CITIES

This extends the demand for the 'right to the city' to the universal 'right to the space'. A complex society is reflected in the brothel in the city centre and the lunch table in the district centre. It manifests itself not only in the temples of high culture on cultural miles, but also permeates every space in an Anthropocene manner. Participation, involvement in spatial decisions, and co-determination are not official acts and dreary compulsory exercises, but basic values of a society that puts its most valuable asset, the design of living space, into collaborative hands.

The clean-up work that the industrial age has left us with in terms of ecological and planning issues is frightening and overwhelming. Only if we approach it socially, across municipalities and comprehensively, will a new image of the region emerge that will finally also mentally tear down the city walls that were the first physical victims of industrialisation.

Overcoming the urban-rural contrast, regional awareness, the closing of material and energy cycles, the end of living and working are the fruits of this cheerful utopia. The possibility for this is the valuable inheritance and are the techniques of the industrial age and their dialectic sublation.

Andreas Hofer was a member of the international jury for EUROPAN 16. He is the director of the International Building Exhibition in Stuttgart 2027 (Internationale Bauausstellung 2027 StadtRegion Stuttgart).

CARE

LIVING CITIES

Elke Krasny

In the 21st century, 'care' has emerged as a new key word. We may think of pandemic care, planetary care, earth care or soil care. Care indicates the urgency and the emergency that people find themselves in to guarantee all the life-sustaining practises needed for futurity. In 2015, Angelika Fitz and myself started to think about architecture and care and how care can be mobilised as a new lens in order to understand the practise of architecture.

Architecture, as the architectural historian, theorist and practising architect Peggy Diemer has stated, is the history of capital. Therefore, architecture has, of course, always also been entangled with what we call today the Anthropocene, Capitalcene and climate catastrophe. Therefore, architecture has a very specific responsibility to find new ways of producing, using materials and making sure that the environment will no longer be destroyed by architecture.

[1] Joan C. Tronto & Berenice Fisher. 'Towards a Feminist Theory of Caring'. In Emily K. Abel & Margaret K. Nelson (eds.), *Circles of Care: Work and Identity in Women's Lives*, Albany, NY: SUNY Press, 1990, pp. 36–54.

Back in 1990, the feminist political scientist and care ethicist Joan Tronto, together with Berenice Fisher, defined what care is in a very broad sense. They wrote: 'In the most general sense, care is a spacious activity that includes everything that we do to maintain, continue and repair our world so that we can live in it as well as possible. That world includes our bodies, ourselves and our environment, all of which we seek to interweave in a complex, life-sustaining web'.[1] What we can gather from this quote is that architecture can best be understood as sitting between the environment which it becomes part of and therefore has a very high impact on the climate and climate change, and of course, preventing climate change and the climate catastrophe. And on the other hand, as our protective and care-taking agency, enabling production for human beings with architecture, protecting humans and giving them shelter. Therefore, the quote that Joan Tronto and Berenice Fisher wrote more than three decades ago makes it possible to judge architecture in order to find out whether it is good at giving care both to the environment and to human beings.

Elke Krasny is a curator, cultural theorist, urban researcher, and writer. She is a professor at the Academy of Fine Arts Vienna. Together with Angelika Fitz, she edited *Critical Care. Architecture and Urbanism for a Broken Planet* (The MIT Press, 2019).

THESES FOR A VIABLE CITY

LIVING CITIES

Elisabeth Merk

Why are people drawn to the cities?

The growth of cities around the world remains unbroken — despite all the problems that advancing urbanisation entails. At the same time, the urgent challenges of climate change, mobility and digitalisation present cities with major transformation tasks. These must be addressed by society as a whole if the changeover to a CO_2-neutral city is to succeed. The city must be viewed as part of the solution, because this is where innovations arise, this is where the structures are found that first make it possible to work on the issues together. The focus must not be placed exclusively on the technical and functional solution approaches but must rather centre on the social questions of justice and thus give preference to strategies that can counteract the spatial disparities.

If the urbanisation trend continues, by 2050 almost 70% of humanity will be living in cities. In Germany, around 77% of the population already lived in cities in 2020, whilst in Austria it was around 59%.

As we know only too well, it would be wrong to believe that Western countries and thus Europe could continue to outsource the necessary transformation processes to maintain the quality of life in their cities in the usual way. Large migration movements in recent decades have shown us that we, as a European community, must overtake mutual responsibility and that national interests can only be viable for the future if we cooperate.

Why, then, this digression on which a city, a city planning councillor, supposedly seems to have no influence?

In the end, it is a question of our common values, which are reflected in the strategic decisions on urban development and likewise manifest in the individual approach to urban concepts on site.

> World population 7,952,348,931
> Germany 83,758,929
> Austria 9,047,076

Decisions that we make today for Munich, Germany or the EU countries always have a global impact — on everyone. Conversely, this means that responsibility must be multiplied by eight billion people.

Vibrant cities worth living in are created because people accept responsibility and tie their dreams, wishes and hopes to the respective place where they want to live, because they expect to generate future prospects for themselves and their families. In return, they are willing to make their energy, their labour and their ideas available.
Let's make something out of them!

The most important challenge for me, therefore, is urban redevelopment that takes the above factors into account and develops out from the centre of the cities.

LIVING CITIES

Stop additional land consumption, strengthen and further develop the green infrastructure in the cities.

Do not eliminate disparities between rural and urban areas, but rather reinforce the respective qualities through intelligent cooperation.

Co-creation: designing open processes — with broad co-determination and innovative participatory processes.

Facilitate a city of 'many' through changed governance structures.

Reform land policy to initiate new urban cooperation with the aim of implementing the guiding principles initiated in the Leipzig Charter. Above all, the mixed city, under socio-economic aspects as well as from the innovative, functional perspectives of a new understanding of the productive city.

Recognise the genius of the respective location and draw on local materials and skills to actually shape the transformation in the sense of a circular city.

Enter into an open, fair dialogue globally in order to jointly tackle the challenges.

Intercultural exchange on equal terms is the only way European cities can learn from cities around the world and vice versa.

The transformation of cities opens new qualities for public space, as places of encounter and places of integration, where democracy can be lived and experienced in everyday life.

Understand building culture and beauty as an engine for sustainable urban development.

Elisabeth Merk was a member of the international jury for EUROPAN 16. She has been the City of Munich's Planning Director since 2007.

IF YOU WANT TO LOOK BACK, THEN TO MODERNISM

LIVING CITIES

Bart Lootsma

Why is it that when we think about cities, we still only consider the images of their historical centres, as if they are a metaphor, a pars pro toto of the whole? I'm quite aware of this, as all my life people almost always react with: 'Oh, straight from Amsterdam!' when I confess my city of birth. This is followed by a list of what they themselves found so great about it. These are usually aspects of the historic city centre: the canals, the old alleys, the red-light district, the coffee shops, and the most famous museums. As in other cities that have become overrun by tourists over the last decades, this produces serious problems for their liveability and sustainability – both in terms of their ecological footprint as well as socially. With the exploding real estate prices, city centres have become unaffordable to live in for most of us. City governments have been working hard to reduce this pressure over the last couple of years, trying to take advantage of the COVID crisis.

Maybe I'm more aware of this because this is not my Amsterdam. I was born in what was the outskirts of the city in the thirties, with my back to the old city, with a view over water and swampy land divided by narrow moats. From the bay window of my grandparents' flat I saw how all this was sprayed with sand, ready for further development. In 1961, my mother and I moved into one of the first of the thousands of flats that were built there. Even as a child I loved the view, the special spatiality of Van Eesteren's urban design – far more important than the individual buildings, where space, supported by generous green, flowed on almost unhindered between the rows. People still earned about the same income and, as Bakema suggested, that was underpinned by the flat roofs. Countless children played on the wide pavements. Groups of people stood in circles, talking to each other. In the evening, the characteristic streetlamps between the young plane trees first lit up green, then shone an ever warmer white as the darkness fell. But I still love this endless green space that can transform into anything, over and over again, from water into land, from sand into streets, from huts into houses. The reinvention of nature through landscape architecture, and the creation of a new artificial ecology, was always the starting point. There is both hope and serenity in it. You can still find it today in Buitenveldert, and it's one of the most popular residential areas in Amsterdam.

This may have been for the original residents of the modernist quarters, who finally got apartments of their own after decades of a housing shortage, like we did. A generation just younger, who had still been born in unspoilt historical cities and villages, saw their unhurt world destroyed, and fought against the further destruction of the inner cities. In the nineteen-seventies, urban renewal became the biggest task for architecture and urbanism, and the largest part of architectural professionals was involved in it. That also steered the international debate of architecture and urbanism, as it appears in publications and teaching, largely away from city extensions, away from urban planning, urban design, and landscape architecture. Large scale social and public housing were gradually abandoned in favour of building for the neighbourhood, which meant that housing became increasingly dependent on existing or new local ownership. This paved the way for the more market-driven approaches of the nineteen-nineties. The flat where I grew up was demolished a few years ago, as was the Bijlmermeer, a neighbourhood in the periphery of Amsterdam from the nineteen-seventies where I later returned, which was largely flawed because the protests against destruction of the inner city, in the Nieuwmarktbuurt, delayed the building of a metro line accessing it. Because of the nostalgic appreciation for the inner city, a future was denied.

'The Architecture of the City' became the core issue, and thereby, in the increasingly international discourse, the emphasis was shifted towards the historical city centre as well as the cultural values architecture represents. Issues of social equality were reframed and the importance of landscape architecture as the basis for an urban scheme decreased. There just was no landscape in the historical city centre, right? And thereby the ecological aspect disappeared in the background or was at best reinvented as green roofs and green facades, to be planted by the owners of the houses them-selves. Liberal individualism turned those city centres into places for the rich and for tourists.

If we want to achieve new, living cities today, in the awareness that we live in the Anthropocene, it would be good to reconsider some knowledge that was built up realising the post-Second World War modernist housing schemes, not only when it comes to financing and ownership, the realisation of large quantities of affordable housing, and in particular also when it comes to the incorporation of green in new, carefully designed ecologies. We have to say goodbye to the dichotomy of nature and culture and embrace the city as a metabolism.

Bart Lootsma is a board member of EUROPAN Austria. He is a historian, theoretician, critic, curator and professor for architectural theory at the University of Innsbruck.

DESIGN THE TRANSITION: A FEW NOTES ON AN EMERGING CULTURE

Paola Viganò

Building an urban project, a public space, or a new building today is tremendously different from the past, even from the recent past. Profound transformations have affected our way of living in both the intimate and the collective space of housing, which has become a space for work and for the coexistence of several generations. They have changed the use of open and public space, for which we ask for ever more consistent continuity and inclusivity. We demand the ability to build new relationships with the geography of a place and its landscapes, with the natural soil, its characteristics, and forms. In all these cases, it is a question of rethinking the artificialisation of the world and the legitimacy of what we call 'design' in the age of ecological transition. The results of the EUROPAN Austria competition reflect on these themes and propose interesting positions.

On the one hand, some projects abandon architecture as traditionally defined, and focus on aspects related to the enhancement of the living: green projects, water, and trees. It is a first sign of the deep change in perspectives and values which also invests in social practices. These projects not only renew lost relationships but produce living conditions for different species. Architecture, in this proposition, does not save the world, but it helps to define the ways of coexistence between different ones.

A second family of projects tackles the issue of ecology and energy transition, starting from the technical challenges and the role that technology will have in functionally redefining space design. In this case, some of the architectural trends of the 1970s come back to life, when the ability to control the environment in all its parts still seemed possible and was a matter of architecture. Design and metabolism seem to renew their alliance.

The problem of resource rarefaction is also tackled in a different way. There are projects that, with sensitive means and some modesty, intervene in the existing, trying to make sense of the dynamics of densification of built space that are increasingly present in many cities in ways that are not trivial. In this case, it is the relationship with the existing that poses a problem; there is the need to clarify its asset value, also in terms of embodied energy. Beyond the traditional idea of restoring selected monuments, today it is a question of addressing the extended urban stratification, a process that allows the city to be rethought and adapted, starting from each single building and in its entirety. The process of adding and erasing will characterise the architectural work in the future and some projects will find a way to show the creativity that can still be put in this exercise on the palimpsest.

Finally, there are also projects that do not seem to consider the distress and criticism of the architectural tradition that goes through the previous positions. We could define these projects as 'out of time'; however, some of them contain a hypothesis that I believe we should not lose sight of. Design is also the ability to draw, to compose a new entity out of heterogeneous objects made up of spatial, linguistic, and material relationships. These projects seem to say, even if with outdated choices and languages, that space and its design matter, not only in detail, but throughout the scales, until the urban and territorial project.

LIVING CITIES

Ecology, technology, and stratifications are all extremely interesting and fundamental approaches to the socio-economic and ecological transition; but the question of space and its quality remains crucial for the outcome of a design activity. Spatial quality (a complex concept that should be considered for its social, ecological, and economic impact) and the emerging culture of the transition have not yet found a common centre, but the projects we have discovered and discussed have been an interesting synthesis of possible directions.

Paola Viganò was a member of the international jury for EUROPAN 16. She is an architect and urbanist, and professor at the EPFL (Lausanne) and IUAV University Venice. She is director of Studio Paola Viganò.

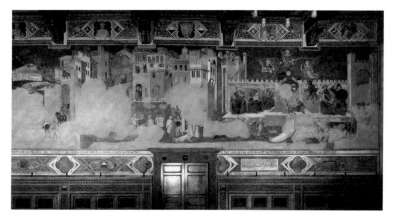

Ambrogio Lorenzetti, *The Allegory of Good and Bad Government*, Sala dei Nove, Palazzo Pubblico, Siena, 1338–1339

1. *Effects of Good Government in the City*
2. *Effects of Good Government in the Country*
3. *Effects of Bad Government in the City*
4. *Effects of Bad Government in the Country*

Source: Wikimedia Commons, Public Domain

THE ROOM OF PEACE (SIENA)

LIVING CITIES

Early in the fourteenth century, Italian painter Ambrogio Lorenzetti painted a fresco commissioned by a board of 'citizen-rulers', comprised of 'good and lawful merchants' of the city-republic of Siena, as a political statement and a premise for a possible future. The room in which it was painted, the Sala dei Nove, was named after the group of nine citizens who were chosen at random to rule the city for the period of six months. At the time of Lorenzetti's commission, this mode of governance, the precedent to our democratic governing, had only recently been established. In the Sala dei Nove, also known as the Room of Peace, Lorenzetti painted a panorama of Siena as one with the surrounding countryside. He painted the city and the countryside twice; first as an imaginary outcome of 'bad governance' in the scene on the west wall known as *The City Under Tyranny (La città-Stato sotto la tirannide)*. Across the room, on the east wall, he portrayed the prospects of 'good governance' or *The Good City-Republic (La buona città-Repubblica)*. The room was therefore the nerve centre of the Sienese republic and the pictorial bible of their republican tradition. It was meant to have a profound aesthetic and didactic effect, reminding the council that the city's faith was in their hands.

The series of photographs portrays the Room of Peace and the fresco in multiple dimensions — the interior views, fragments, and materiality. In the work, the fresco is placed in the context of the Room, the Palace, and the city, but also shown in its pictorial elements and details. The intimate relation of the painted image and architectural space, rare in contemporary architecture, is a precious theme. Through the narrative tool of framing, the work creates an open script, a new description of the Sala della Pace and *The Allegory of Good and Bad Governance*, mirroring the themes of the contemporary urban world, urban governance, and representation in our time.

Bas Princen is an artist and architectural photographer living and working in Rotterdam and Zurich. The installation 'The Room Of Peace (Siena)' shown on previous pages, was exhibited at the 14th Venice Architecture Biennale 2014.

ENTRIES AND AWARDEES
IN TOTAL

REGISTRATIONS 1102

WINNERS 40

ENTRIES 677

SHORTLIST 201

PRIZES 127
SPECIAL MENTIONS 46

RUNNERS-UP 41

WINNERS 40

TRADING THE BIG AND THE SMALL

GRAZ

SCALE
- urban and architectural

LOCATION
Graz, Austria

POPULATION
291,072 inhabitants

STUDY SITE
15.1 ha

PROJECT SITE
7,370 m²

ACTORS
CITYPARK Graz,
City of Graz

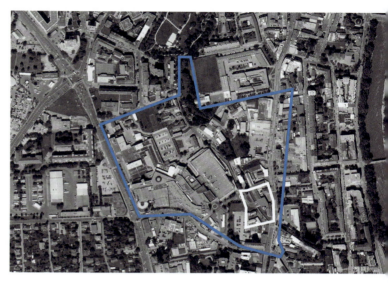

strategic site
project site

Shopping malls are to be found on the outskirts of town. Atypically, the 'CITYPARK' in Graz, a substantial shopping agglomeration from the 1970s, with parking garages and accompanying streetscape, is located in a truly central spot. Due to its expansive volume and its focus on cars, the complex appears as somewhat of an 'alien giant' sitting in a neighbourhood of much smaller scale. The shopping mall area will be transformed substantially within the next few years. According to the zeitgeist back then, the building was oriented towards the major arterial road, the Lazarettgürtel – making it easily accessible for cars. Its huge demand for individual parking spaces was met by a multi-storey garage, located on the presumed 'back side' of the mall area and creating a separation from the city. Today, with the focus on slow mobility, public transport, and a change in people's shopping behaviour, the owners of the mall understand the need to transform. They recognise the potential of the former 'back side' as the new interface with the city. Thus, the multi-storey garage will be replaced by underground parking, allowing for an inviting gesture on the ground floor that opens the area towards the city. Moreover, mere shopping is envisaged to give way to a mix of trade, commerce, and production, as well as residential living and education. Sketched out is a future scenario of a truly mixed city and a lively, enjoyable environment – characterised by ingredients most new developments would claim as their own. So far, so good, so predictable. Why, then, does this place of special interest contain a potential to think up new urban constellations?

Firstly, it poses the question of how to fruitfully combine a capitalist machine with everyday living – more specifically – with an everyday living intended to be socially inclusive. In recent years, societal standards and guarantees have become brittle and the current pandemic has deepened this situation. Shopping for the sake of satisfying superficial needs, as evoked by advertisements, is not common practice anymore. Today, immersed in digital habits, we research product ratings before buying, we are aware of a product's origin and mode of production. As responsible consumers, we are more hesitant, more conscious, and more responsible, all this being a threat for a temple of consumerism. However, with circumstances changing, a window of opportunity opens where society warms to the idea of venturing into new behaviours, seemingly only waiting for interesting scenarios to be offered. Returning to the EUROPAN 16 site, we find several lucky coincidences that meet here: The owner of a mall is conscious of the situation and interested in change. He offers a concrete site to act, which is placed on a pivotal spot within an area of great transformation. Key aspects for the development of a district where profit interest meets everyday life need to be negotiated. Can the nature of future shopping behaviour be instrumentalised to generate spin-off uses that support the community, as well as the CITYPARK? Can the role of the future shopping centre be envisaged to act as an enabler and a general motor providing a solid infrastructure for new components and test scenarios on a wider scale and spatial dimension?

Secondly, we encounter an adjacent, grown neighbourhood area, which is also currently changing through densification. Many new housing projects have been realised recently, bringing more people to the area. Formerly empty spaces between existing housing blocks have been closed, resulting in a continuous, urban street front. Located on the southern corner of this development and south of the EUROPAN site is Karlauplatz. Nondescript and essentially used for parking and traffic today, the square seems tucked away. Upon closer examination, its spatial qualities and urban potential reveal themselves. The church, the abandoned traditional bakery, the figurative Marian Column featuring the Virgin Mary and several saints, and the Mühlgang creek are reminiscent of a historic village centre. Small-scale slowness and communal living are now overwritten by urban bustle. A damaged fabric waits to regain its identity and divulge its original strength to provide a sense of place for its inhabitants.

Another important ingredient, most relevant to establish a healthy and liveable city, is the fact that the site is surrounded by remarkable green spaces. Branching from there, a patchy network of nature weaves into the area. In fact, crossing the site is a mill stream, an agent for nature. Its currently sealed riverbanks hold a possibility to activate one of the most precious elements for inclusive use a city may have: a resilient base enhancing the urban quality for humans and non-humans alike and mediating between different urban interests.

A tram line also crosses through, anchoring a public mobility axis in the quarter. Tram stops will set the frame for urban places. A mix of resources are at hand and want to be instrumentalised for a coherent and inclusive concept to emerge. At the centre is the E16 site. Its role will be to negotiate and to synergise, thereby weaving all the parts together. Its bridging function will not only be of a spatial manner; it will additionally need to mediate the social and the digital by interpreting future commerce strategies and valorising the local potential.

Bridge crossing Mühlgang, with the project site on the right and the view towards the north

GRAZ

GRAZ

OPENING GRUEN'S BOX: CIVIC PROSPECTS IN GRAZ

Akil Scafe-Smith

Towards the end of the 1970's, the infamous 'father of the shopping mall', Victor Gruen, permanently retreated from the United States to his home city of Vienna. Disillusioned with his legacy, disavowing of his architectural enfant terrible, and near distant from his eventual death in 1980, Gruen was ostensibly on his way out in more ways than one. Meanwhile, the grand behemoth of 'Shopping City Süd', still the largest mall in Austria today, was very much on its way in. The mall, originally contrived as a *deus ex machina* for the civic regeneration of the North American suburbs and then turned into a wayward mechanism for capital investment by US congressional changes in 1954, became a haunting apparition in Gruen's last years: a Pandora's box ajar, from which the celebrated émigré architect had lost sight of hope.

What Gruen would have thought of Graz's own 'giant shopping machine', the 'CITYPARK', built in 1971 before Vienna's Shopping City Süd, could well have been on the minds of many built environment professionals in the city at the time. Unlike many malls, CITYPARK is anything but suburban. The mall is located in the *Stadtbezirk* of Gries, one of the city's densest municipal districts. Above it is the fabled neighbourhood of Annenviertel, an ambiguously defined haven of migration and activity, and also home to Graz's red-light district. Surrounding it are pointedly urban ecological territories. To the east, the Mühlgang, a canalised diversion from the River Mur that briefly fed an artist-led swimming pool project in 2003. To the north, Oeversee Park, a participatorily planned green space financed and delivered under the *Platz für Menschen* initiative by the EU programme, URBAN Graz. All of these beautifully complex contextual parts are then compounded by what the CITYPARK site owner, perhaps an unknowingly contemporary Gruenian thinker himself, once called in passing the importance of the mall's 'sociological aspect'. I have indeed myself experienced the gently moving tide of social life in the mall. Readily apparent are the flotsam and jetsam of young people and families who convene there not to buy but to be, sauntering through the CITYPARK caverns with a remarkably 'downtown' conviviality: Gruen's great unfulfilled desire for the spaces he would ultimately label 'bastard developments'.

Of course, none of these quite delicate urban intrigues instinctively 'balance the books' for what is fundamentally a revenue-generating enterprise. And so, in the advent of great global changes to how we as a society consume, CITYPARK is hoping to undergo changes of a concomitant magnitude. This sets the scene for an incredibly exciting, if not daunting, EUROPAN 16 site, which is nestled at the stimulated interface of the mall and the surrounding city. Though small, the site is itself almost moving; intersected by a variety of infrastructures of movement such as the tramline, the Mühlgang, a pedestrian and cycle route called the Brückengasse, and the roads leading out of the mall. The site has naturally inherited the urban entanglements of CITYPARK, but importantly, not its destiny. Unfettered by an underlying need to generate revenue, which perhaps gives rise to the site's difficulty and, frankly, reveals the need for an area-wide masterplan in the near future, the site is indeed an extraordinary example of the living city and an opportunity to seriously consider the competition's themes of metabolic and inclusive vitalities.

In light of this, the sites' three runners-up have all made extremely courageous attempts at addressing the site through architectural intervention.

Superstructure Urban Solution illustrated an equal part dystopian-utopian vision of how modern spaces of production must be understood as part and parcel of our cities, bringing urban-level waste management and recycling processes into the domestic sphere. *Post-Shopping* channelled the spirits of 60's megastructural folly but with a certain urban intelligence that acknowledged the explicitly urban scale of the task at hand. *Free Mühlgang* boasted a radical appropriation of the canal, showcasing a vision that addressed how inclusivity of both human difference and that-which-is-different to humans is inextricable from an equitable urban future.

However, there were a number of perceived aporias in the three proposals, owing again to the difficulty that such a site posed. Consequently, as the jury, we recommended that the shortlisted teams partner for the implementation process, which I understood as not only an intuitive decision but also one that followed the spirit of the EUROPAN competition. Though each proposal posited brave conceptual responses, the projects individually lacked what the collective exhibited. As such, it would have been to express a sincere lack of awareness of the competition's war cry – asking how radical new possibilities for 'living cities' might allow us to live together – for the jury not to suggest some means of the competition's most notable entries to coexist, bettering one another and opening up exciting new collaborative avenues. It is on this final note also that a last invocation of Gruen's solemn spectre would be a timely one. For whatever the Pandoran figure would have thought about CITYPARK, it can be almost certain that he would have viewed the civic possibilities for the EUROPAN 16 site, enabled by this exciting collaboration, with hope.

Akil Scafe-Smith was a member of the international jury for EUROPAN 16. He is one sixth of RESOLVE, an interdisciplinary design collective that aims to address multi-scalar social challenges by combining architecture, art, technology and engineering.

INTERVIEW WITH THE SITE PARTNERS

What are the main questions posed to the competitors concerning the transformation of the site?
Martin Poppmeier: Our shopping centre is fifty years old, a grown structure that has organically evolved and needs to continue to do so to successfully persevere through current, challenging market trends. We face general changes in shopping habits and on a more local level we see changes in our immediate neighbourhood, which is growing strongly. Once the ongoing construction and development projects that have progressed to final planning stages will finish, nearly one thousand new apartments will be completed within the next few years. Our goal is to become an integral part of this expanding neighbourhood. Moreover, we want to become a vital player supporting visionary programmatic ideas and connecting with them.
The location of the E16 site is really the key to help accomplish that. It will be a crucial mosaic stone that links the shopping centre and the surrounding developments. We are asking for ideas that can attract a mixed range of people from different backgrounds and professions and function as the 'glue' that will bring it all together.

How is the site linked to the two subtopics of 'metabolism' and 'inclusivity'?
Wilfried Krammer: The City of Graz is interested in seeing wider-scaled concepts for public space that tackle connectivity and highlight existing values, thus establishing a framework for the entire area. It is particularly about connecting nearby green areas, emphasising the presence of the on-site Mühlgang (mill stream), bringing the old and new together and creating places with a quality of stay for everyone. Plans for a tramline crossing the site will additionally enhance the human scale in the currently car-dominated area by accentuating the presence of natural components, improving easy accessibility, and focussing on landscape architecture. Especially with a view towards networking the diverse contents of the adjoining urban spaces, we are ambitiously striving towards a metabolic and inclusive city quarter.

Have you already defined a specific process for the territorial and/or urban and/or architectural development of the site after the EUROPAN competition? Do you expect a proposal from the competitors linked to what they proposed in their prize-winning projects?

Martin Poppmeier: From the outset, our aim for participating in EUROPAN has been to trigger new ideas from a young, international architectural community for a challenging design task, hoping that we may even find a solution we can realise in our greater development plans. These encompass a much larger space, which includes the shopping centre, and also directly affect our neighbours and the adjacent traffic system. These farther-reaching implications have led to a more time-consuming process than expected, but we cannot reasonably determine the further steps until we complete them. At this point, we also do not want to request further proposals from the prize winners. However, we are interested in keeping the awarded ideas as valuable input in the overall process. The first meetings with the winning teams are already planned.

Martin Poppmeier is a EUROPAN 16 site representative for the site in Graz. He is the owner of the project site.

Wilfried Krammer is a EUROPAN 16 site representative for the City of Graz. He is a project manager at the Executive Office for Urban Planning, Development and Construction, where he is responsible for the revitalisation of the CITYPARK/Gries area.

Brückengasse and
Mühlgang crossing the
project site, view
towards the north

GRAZ   RUNNER-UP   44

POST-SHOPPING

What if we analyse the urban ethos of Graz? What if we use the urban breeding ground of the city itself as a prototype for the site, as a recipe that orders the urban ingredients of a prosumer-oriented shopping mall?

The project is intended to be developed in time, constructing a series of infrastructural corridors that enable prosumer-oriented activities to be injected into CITYPARK.

These architectural spines, these infrastructures, do not just allow the connection between both sides of the CITYPARK, but also introduce and articulate a series of complementary activities, hosted within architectural pieces, that hybridise the consumer-oriented ethos of the shopping mall with many other types of non-commercial programmes.

PRIZE
Runner-Up

PROJECT
Post-Shopping

AUTHORS
Pedro Pitarch Alonso (ES)
Architect

Pedro Pitarch
Architectures & Urbanisms
Madrid

pedropitarch.com
@pedropitarch

This strategy allows the CITYPARK to become a public active space for citizens, where production and consumption overlap.

Moreover, the new CITYPARK's living room is more than a building; it becomes the core, the social heart of the wider masterplan for the CITYPARK. As well as the urban gate that defines a transition, a migration from the domestic ethos of the surrounding area, to the commercial and public ethos of the New Post-Shopping CITYPARK.

'The site offers a unique context to rethink the role of architects in the contemporary city by defining a critical framework from which to reinvent conventional architectural typologies, such as the shopping mall, and to transform them into social condensers of cultural and economic innovation.

The project is neither a plaza nor a building but something in between. A place amidst urbanism and architecture. A common framework for social gathering, cultural exchange and dialogue. The project stands as the transformation of the site into an urban living room that mediates the migration from "consumer-oriented" practices into "prosumer-oriented" ones'.

GRAZ RUNNER-UP 46

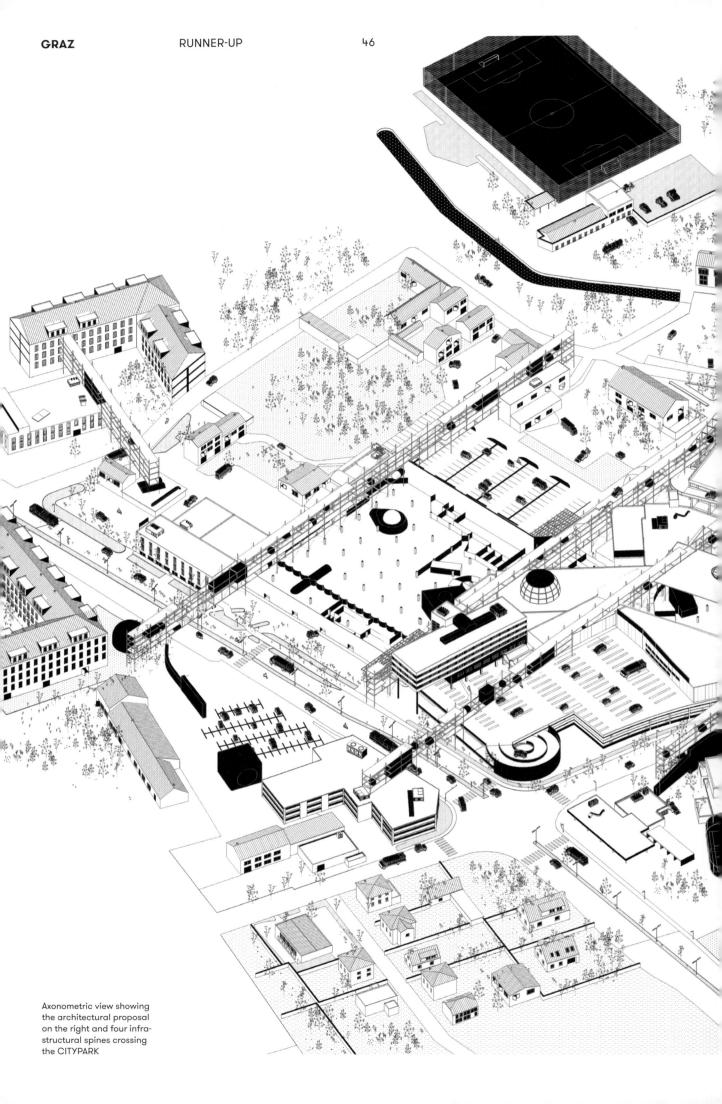

Axonometric view showing the architectural proposal on the right and four infrastructural spines crossing the CITYPARK

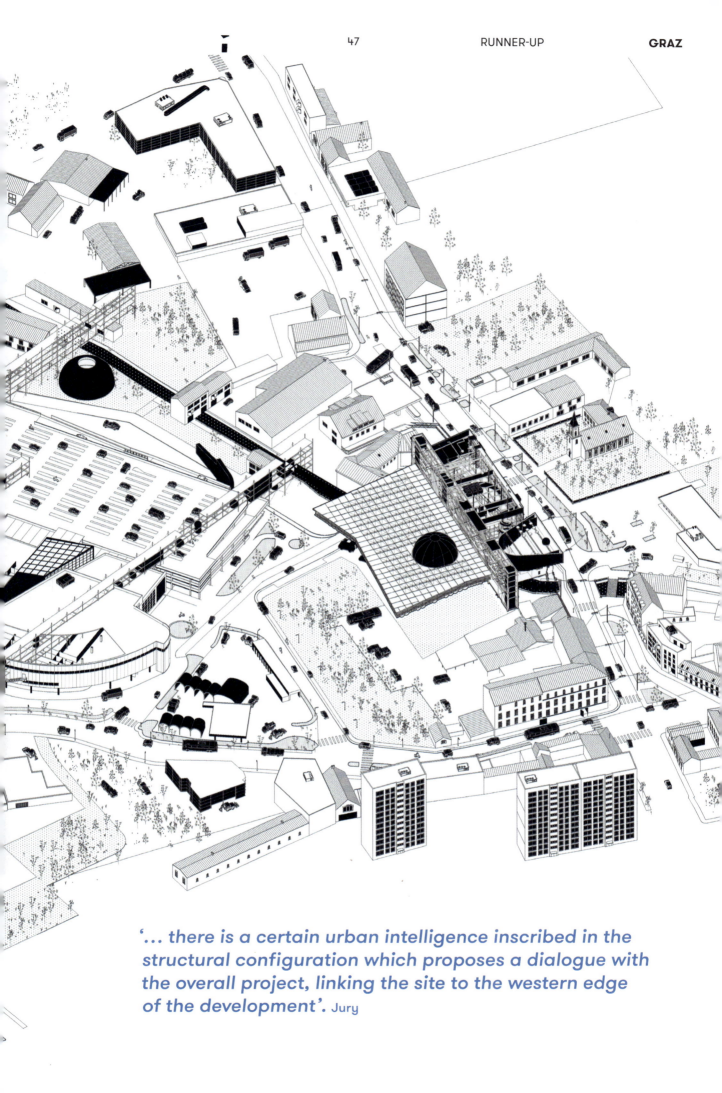

'... there is a certain urban intelligence inscribed in the structural configuration which proposes a dialogue with the overall project, linking the site to the western edge of the development'. Jury

GRAZ RUNNER-UP 48

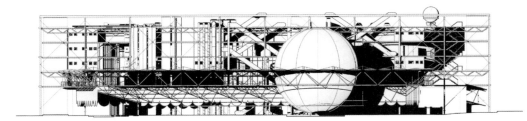

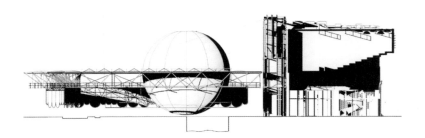

The proposed project is understood as an architectural device, creating infinite types of spaces for cultural production and consumption. It functions rather as a machine than as a conventional building. Its author calls it a 'social condenser', designed with a capability to trigger functions that would construct cultural, social, and metropolitan contexts, surrounding its main programme, a concert hall, and extending it to further realms.

Top left:
Section west-east axis
Centre left:
Section north-south axis
Bottom left:
Ground floor plan
Right:
Axonometric view, from below

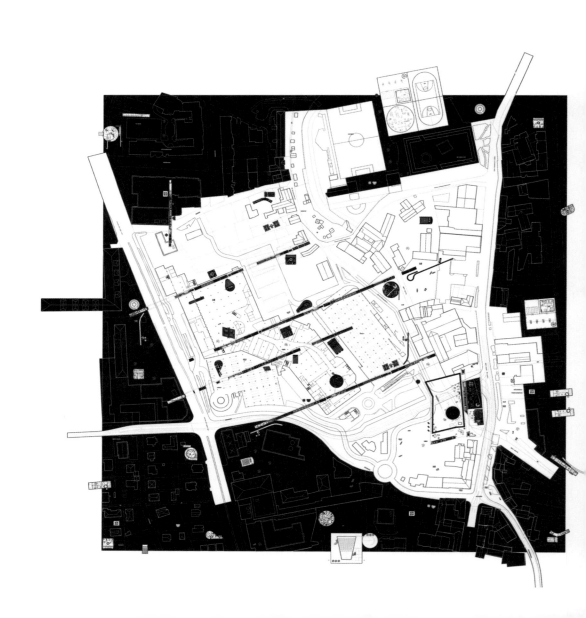

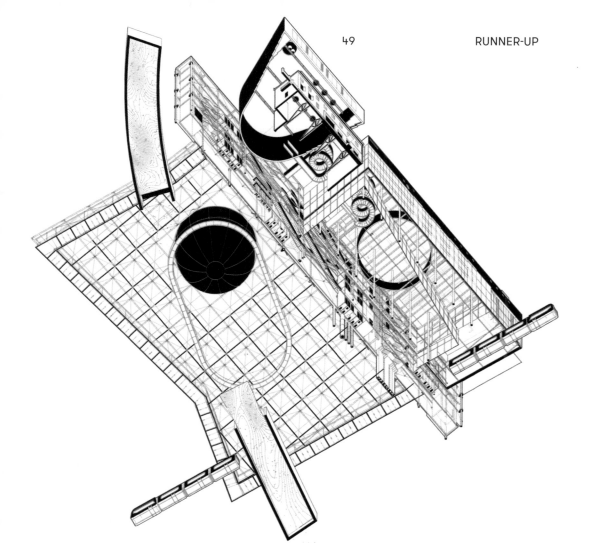

JURY STATEMENT

The aesthetically very pleasing character presented through beautiful drawings is a skill set that was highly valued by the jury. Nevertheless, a contradictory discussion evolved: Is the proposal feasible in an era of climate crises? What about the maintenance concept of the proposed convention centre and its gigantic square? What about its anachronistic touch: Such megastructures were conceived decades ago. Should we accept them nowadays? Parts of the jury see a glorification of a certain architectural language from the 1980s paired with the 1960s belief in megastructures as a large-scaled hardware that shall create collectivity. Especially in the context of the E16 theme *Living Cities*, the jury critically discusses whether such an approach could provide a relevant answer.

On the other hand, members of the jury hint to particular qualities. Concerning its appearance to the Griesgasse, the proposal creates the most convincing urban image amongst all the projects. It is appreciated as interesting for its scale and design. It solves the problem of the facade, the relationship to the church and it has a strong interface.

It is not a modest thing, though. Moreover, there is a certain urban intelligence inscribed in the structural configuration which proposes a dialogue with the overall project, linking the site to the western edge of the development. The intervention is clearly overdone and programmed far too densely. Nevertheless, the concept of an ambitious reading of the urban potential, based in an intense dialogue between the EUROPAN site and the overall development area, remains as a quality to be respected and integrated in the future development. Thus, the proposal reflects a larger urban context, involving the important street at the other side of the shopping centre by linear infrastructures, with flexible plug-in programmes that provide a future opportunity for connectivity.

In general, the approach of linking the suburb to the 'world of the shopping centre', its new development and its beyond, is recognised as a value to be addressed in the future development strategy.

GRAZ　　　RUNNER-UP　　　50

FREE MÜHLGANG

'Free Mühlgang' unburies the traces of the past to reveal, through a process of erosion, the stories, events, and people(s) that have been forgotten, excluded, and silenced. Through the materialisation of new programmes and exchanges, we will honour them and connect them to the present. From the territorial perspective, we propose to liberate the Mühlgang, recovering it for the city and its citizens, whilst reasserting the significance of this unique urban element through an inclusive public green-blue corridor. The proposal – a wetland landscape 'Waterever' and an elevated thermae 'Hinge' – becomes a statement for an inclusive architecture, which involves and integrates a wide range of actors that will inhabit, discover, transform, and enhance a new vision for Gries and the city of Graz.

'Since our first encounter with the site, we were intrigued by its complexity, tensions, and potential, and by the diversity of cultures coexisting in Gries. We were also fascinated by Mühlgang's history and became passionate about unburying its past traces. Liberating the Mühlgang from its current containment, we created a playful wetland to support its own urban and wildlife. Revisiting the Roman thermae, we defined a permeable elevated gateway to house an inclusive programme based on environmental awareness, alternative modes of consumption, gender equality, and LGTB identity development'.

JURY STATEMENT

The jury highlights the careful analysis and the new perspective on metabolism in the city. The way the project traces the layers of history and relates them to the site is interesting, studying the potential meaning of the canal in relation to its social and ecological values. For the site's urban ground, the team proposes a heterotopic public space whose atmosphere, topography, and form are defined by its dynamic relation to water/flooding. To transform the canal into an intense physical dialogue with water is seen as a contemporary approach to new forms of public space. Compared to other projects, which use the Mühlgang in a mere functional way, this proposal highlights the aesthetic, emotional, and atmospheric component of water, adding important qualities which rightfully challenge the design of public space.

While it is highly appreciated that the project works with the force of water, giving it a new meaning and a destination within the city, it is also critically questioned whether the natural power of the flood and the forces of flowing water are captured in its complexity. The Mühlgang is an artificial canal and not a wild river. The lack of a deeper examination of water flows and riverbed conditions has resulted in the articulation of a rather formal landscape design. Instead of working with the forces of water, the layout of the curved lines unfortunately obscures how a dynamic relation with water expansion and water reduction could be translated into a credible landscape design.

On a programmatic level, the project expands the water discourse, emphasising social, ecological, and educational aspects that also emerge from the analysis. Its explicit specificity of possible uses is recognised as a clear statement about the site as an in-between identity, which can neither be directly linked to the mechanism of suburban upgrading nor to the redevelopment logics of the new shopping centre-neighbourhood itself. It creates a kind of autonomous third place which, at the same time, is a highly inclusive open space.

PRIZE
Runner-Up

PROJECT
Free Mühlgang

AUTHORS
Violeta Ordóñez Manjón (ES)
Architect
Raquel Ruiz García (ES)
Architect
Mónica Lamela Blázquez (ES)
Architect

Madrid, Los Angeles
@freemuehlgang
@monicalamela
@raquelruiz.arch

Right:
Visualisation of ground floor plan showing the wetland landscape 'Waterever' with cross section and facade of the 'Hinge' building

GRAZ RUNNER-UP 52

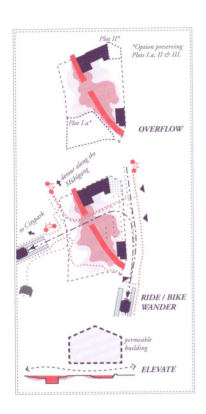

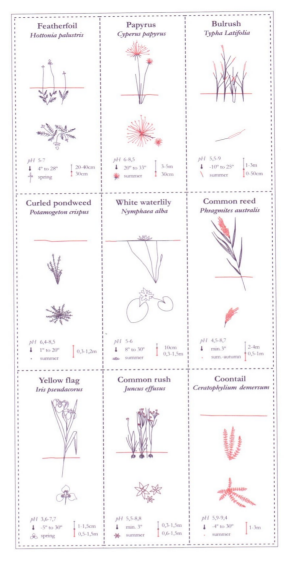

Top left:
Urban strategy

Top right:
Catalogue of floating and ornamental-filtering aquatic plants of the wetland ecosystem

Right:
The project emerges from a territorial reading of the social, historical, and cultural context that frames it. In a process of 'Erosion' traces of the past are revealed.

The complex analysis on the right shows the re-envisioned corridor along the Mühlgang through its historic time-periods.

GRAZ RUNNER-UP

'To transform the canal into an intense physical dialogue with water is seen as a contemporary approach to new forms of public space'. Jury

RUNNER-UP　　　GRAZ

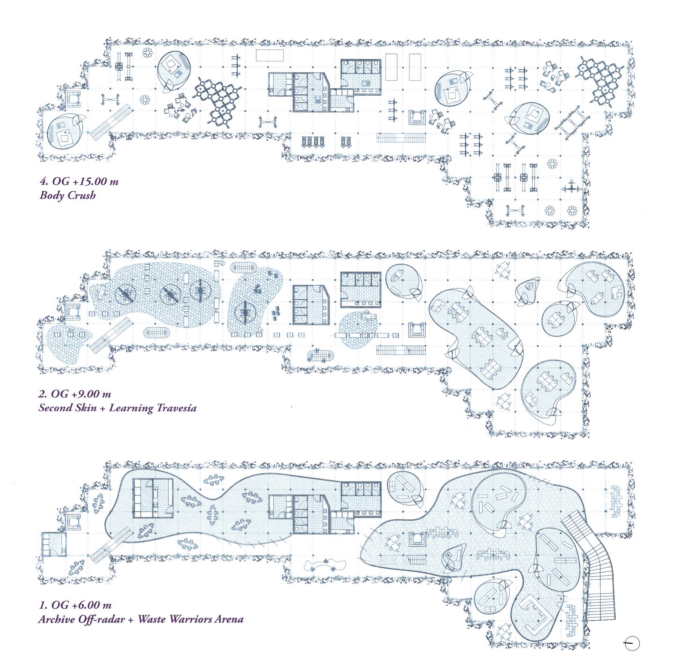

4. OG +15.00 m
Body Crush

2. OG +9.00 m
Second Skin + Learning Travesía

1. OG +6.00 m
Archive Off-radar + Waste Warriors Arena

Left:
Visualisation of the 'Hinge' a permeable building with a green facade that extends the landscape upwards. It derives from the notion of the 'thermae' in ancient Rome, where people would gather to socialise around water.

Right:
Floor plans show the functions on different levels, which reflect on the different realities and becomings that coexist in the Gries district. The 'Hinge' is to be understood as a statement for an inclusive architecture, which involves and integrates a wide range of actors.

URBAN SOLUTIONS SUPERSTRUCTURE

PRIZE
Runner-Up

PROJECT
Urban Solutions Superstructure

AUTHOR
Rene Dapperger (DE)
Architect

Studio RMD
Stuttgart

szenarioblog.com
@renemax1

Urban problems require urban solutions. Innovations are desperately needed to keep up with ecological and economic challenges. We have spun a net of superstructures over Graz which will provide exactly that. A decentralised trading net of unique superstructures that provide the urban needs with nourishment, material, and energy. These three parameters are included in every superstructure and traded among themselves to stop the constant import and failed metabolism of global trading. The proposed project on the E16 site – SUPERSTRUCTURE GRAZ SÜD 1 – feeds from the local parameters of PLASTICGOLD (urban mining and recycling) to produce 3D-printed innovations.

'When I first visited the site, I had my car parked only a few blocks from the CITYPARK shopping centre. Walking towards the project site, I was drowned in the sheer unlimited potential of its surroundings. It also became clear to me that this part of the city needed change. So, the project became what I would like to see this area become. A welcoming, but productive, an effective but also heart-warming place.
I was also intrigued by the Mühlgang as I saw a tonne of hidden qualities within the green axis through the site. All in all, the project addresses certain urban problems in a drastic way whilst not forgetting the human dimension and its importance in today's urban architecture. This is also what I am looking forward to in the upcoming process'.

Right:
Visualisation of SUPERSTRUCTURE GRAZ SÜD 1 showing the aquaponic system on 1st floor. In this project aquaponic (level 1 & 3) is combined with living (level 2 & 4) and production of 3D-printed products from recycled plastic (level 5). The energy storage system and research entities are present on all levels. Showrooms, workshops, DIY-print facilities and a distribution hub are located on the ground floor.

'The problem with infrastructure is that its appearance is usually suppressed or expelled from the city'. Jury

GRAZ RUNNER-UP 58

Visualisation of the project
within its neighbourhood

RUNNER-UP **GRAZ**

JURY STATEMENT

The jury appreciates the proposed system for being interesting. The question of how to integrate infrastructure in the city and how to make the process of metabolism visible is clearly addressed here. An intense discussion developed on the issue of contextualisation and if a break in scale could enrich the city.

Clearly, infrastructure always goes beyond the scale of the local. The problem with infrastructure is that its appearance is usually suppressed or expelled from the city. We put it in places where we don't see it, and not in the context of the inner-city fabric. Hence, generally there is hardly any awareness of how daily life is maintained. In this sense, the project could also be read as conveying an educational mission if placed on this site. In line with this argument is the fact that two autonomous structures defined by a geometry of bigness are already in the neighbourhood: the shopping centre and the parking garage. Thus, the area could be exactly the right place for integrating such a project – a next generation of fair technology; the area of a shopping centre might become a new kind of infrastructure device. The project might even need this scale in order to work and become a useful organism.

Whereas some jury members appreciate the project's provocative scale and appearance as an alien landing that triggers fruitful and necessary disruptions in the city, some members of the jury remain very sceptical to the appropriate contextualisation of the project in the urban fabric. They criticise the project's sheer volume, its autistic appearance, its lack of relational scale and mediating elements to the surroundings, the church, the neighbouring buildings, and the public space. They point at the modular structure inherent in the building. Because of this modularity, the project could easily be relocated and reassembled. It could be integrated into the new configuration of the shopping centre, either as an additional layer on top, or it could be converted into a system that integrates itself respectively in the overall future development.

GRAZ RUNNER-UP

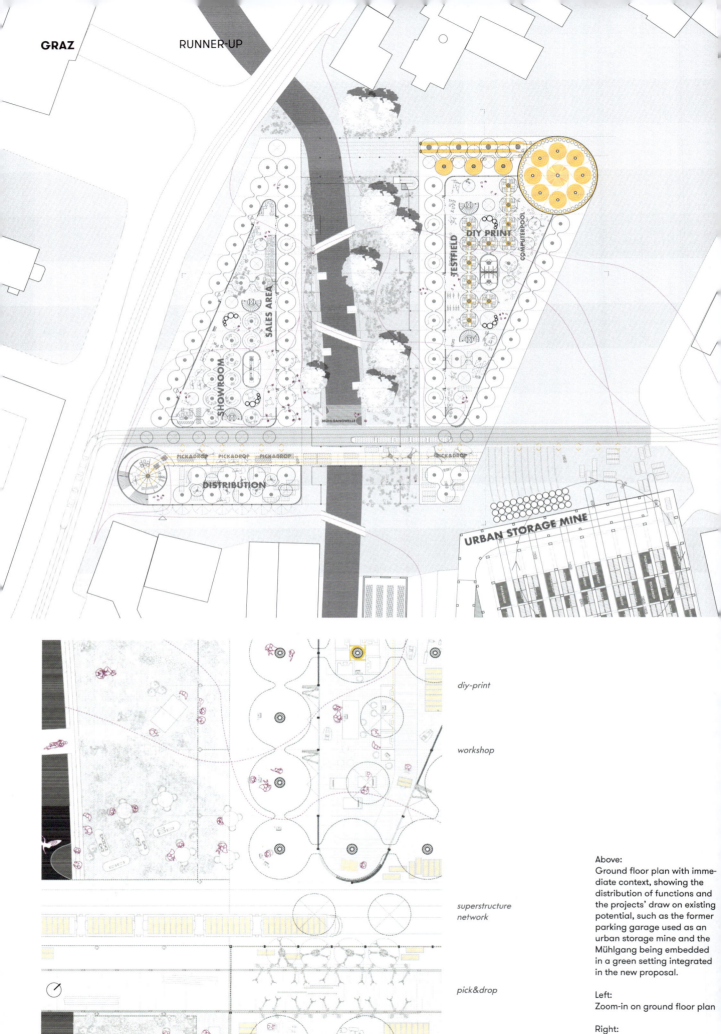

Above:
Ground floor plan with immediate context, showing the distribution of functions and the projects' draw on existing potential, such as the former parking garage used as an urban storage mine and the Mühlgang being embedded in a green setting integrated in the new proposal.

Left:
Zoom-in on ground floor plan

Right:
Axonometric drawing of structural components

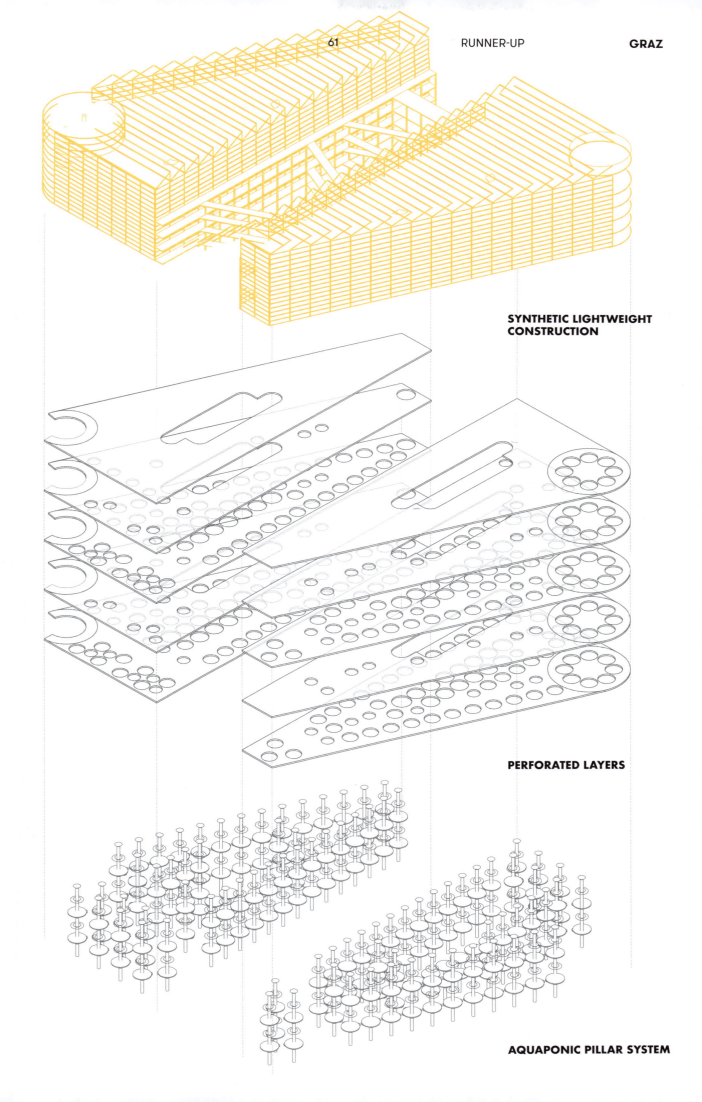

PAR-TICIPANTS' BACK-GROUNDS

ARCHITECTURE 69.5 %

URBAN PLANNER 16.1 %

LANDSCAPE 7.7 %

DESIGN 2.8 %

ENGINEERING 2 %

OTHER 1.8 %

KLAGENFURT

EDUCATING INCLUSIVITY

KLAGENFURT

SCALE
– urban and architectural

LOCATION
Klagenfurt, Austria

POPULATION
101,403 inhabitants

STUDY SITE
72.6 ha

PROJECT SITE
6.1 ha

ACTORS
City of Klagenfurt,
Stadtwerke Klagenfurt,
Klagenfurt Mobil GmbH,
FSF Real Estate,
Chamber of Commerce

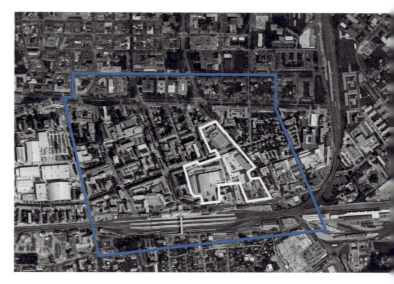

— strategic site
⸺ project site

When thinking about a coexisting future, public infrastructure is a central consideration. Not only in relation to a low carbon footprint, but also in terms of accessibility for all. Depending on the scale and reach, it can connect regions with their urban areas and interlink major cities and countries. A robust and fast grid of connectivity allows action on a wider scale and provides new options of interaction. It is a powerful tool to make cities resilient and inclusive in the future, as it can stimulate exchanges, trigger new influences, and foster diversity. Klagenfurt will soon profit from a new connectivity input, recognised as a great chance on many levels. New possibilities will derive from this endeavour, generating an urban transformation process in the wider area. The E16 site will be its first cornerstone with the potential to ground this unique opportunity. It will serve as a pilot project and will set the frame for a future development.

Klagenfurt is the southernmost regional capital of Austria, on the shores of a large lake. Paired with a continental climate – hot summers and cold winters – it is a popular destination for sports and tourism. For EUROPAN 16, Klagenfurt offers its most important site in the city today. Within the next five years, Klagenfurt will be linked to a superior mobility system. With the soon-to-be completed high-speed southern railway line, the city will enter a new dimension of connectivity. A missing link – long awaited – will close a gap in the Baltic-Adriatic Corridor in Europe. Stretching from north to south, from the Baltic Sea to the Adriatic Sea, it covers 1,700 kilometres of infrastructure. Klagenfurt is one of the stops along this route and will be plugged into an expansive rail network. On a more local level, it will connect two regional capital cities which had previously been three-and-a-half hours apart, now reachable within 45 minutes. The E16 site is at the core of this prospect, located next to the main station.

Infrastructure hubs in themselves are already highly dynamic places in a city. The E16 site is located directly in the vicinity of the train station and on the

KLAGENFURT

route towards the city centre, only a stone's throw away; we could say between the buzz of arrivals and departures and the buzz of a centre inviting people to stay. Wedged between these particularities, the site can be interpreted as an interface that takes advantage of these dynamic places.

Another key characteristic of the site's neighbourhood is the concentration of educational institutions: numerous schools, training facilities, administrative functions and a music university are situated in the area, many of them in need of additional room. Large-scale volumes on site are prone to stimulate uses that provide a nurturing ground for a mixed liveliness. Youth, students, and adults are 'at home' in these streets. Amongst them are people who are about to finish their education or to be re-trained and might be thinking about which future path to take.

The social composition of the area will be vital. Cultural and a maker spaces are already anchored on site. Its educational focus brings the topic of 'new learning' and 'new apprenticeship' to the table. How can learning become multi-dimensional, thereby including all its audiences across professions and ages, and its related uses? What does a spatial expression operating in a synergetic mode for working, living, making, learning, exchanging, and enjoying look like? The quarter asks for typologies where all this can happen simultaneously, where generations and cultures can take care of each other, where spaces can be shared according to current needs and where mentors and mentees can interact. Valorising the buzz from the nearby infrastructure, the proximity to the centre and the potential for a unique use combination will lay another set of opportunities upon the site.

Accessible and equitable infrastructure is a key element to enhance exchange and join a network of broadening (personal and economic) choices. The new, high-speed infrastructure serves as the trigger for this development, attracting different groups of people, both from the city and from further afield. Thus, the site bears the potential of becoming a melting pot of ideas with open exchange being its driving force. The global trend of moving back to cities is also perceptible amongst Carinthians. With travel time reduced dramatically, Klagenfurt will be put on the map for people who value living in healthy surroundings with nature, education, and culture, and at the same time see the chance to have interesting work prospects close by. But it will only thrive if people's different motives, needs, and backgrounds are recognised and seen as valuable sources to be included in a development aiming to arrive at a shared togetherness – a stimulating place to live.

Scenic bus depot halls with adjacent garage building, view towards the east

WHERE WILL ALL THE BUSES GO?

KLAGENFURT

Benni Eder

Over time, living cities and their urban infrastructures need to change to stay alive. Especially at the fringes of historical urban cores, we can observe how formerly outsourced public infrastructures like workshops, cemeteries, stockyards, and in the case of Klagenfurt, bus depots and garages, now become relevant actors of urban regeneration. Depending on the local context, this particular urban equipment might vary its location, scale, performance, change its very nature, or disappear entirely from our urban territories. If approached strategically and with a long-term vision, these mutations represent opportunities and potentials to facilitate and structure necessary transformations of our cities. In fact, Klagenfurt already handled several well-orchestrated urban transformations. But it is becoming increasingly evident that our communities must utilise more opportunities on multiple scales to tackle the difficulties and challenges of today.

The E16 site with its strategic location in between Klagenfurt's main station and the historical city centre surrounded by major educational institutions represents an exceptional opportunity to establish a strong link between these important urban realms. At present, the project site is closed off from the surrounding neighbourhood, but the overall approach for this area, formulated in the city's urban development plan 2020+, already underlines a clear commitment to porosity, connectivity, and soft mobility. Perhaps looking closer at the existing resources on-site and building on what's 'already there' would complement this strategy, transforming the accumulation of heterogeneous elements including a former tramway remise and a city bus depot, into an outstanding example of a resilient and mixed-use 'Liveable City'.

Partly located inside the strategic site we find a notable result of a structural urban transformation the city is still profiting from — Klagenfurt's 'Ring'. It occupies the area of the former fortification around the city's historical core and embodies a coexistence of high-quality public spaces, old built heritage, new infrastructures, manifold programmes, natural elements, monuments, and contemporary structures. The 'Ring' represents a heterogeneous as well as generous urban space that connects the historical centre with the surrounding city extensions.

So the central question is how to refine this urban culture of coexistence and complexity present in the city of Klagenfurt and, to a certain extent, already existing inside the project site itself? The primary success of this EUROPAN 16 competition is that clear and imaginable answers are formulated in the prize-winning projects. Enhancing and implementing these viable approaches will perhaps be challenging but it will release outstanding opportunities for the evolution of the city as well as for the winning team.

The runner-up project 'Tracing Domains' delivers a clear concept of how to orchestrate the different implementation phases and step-by-step unlock the hidden potentials of the site. The renovation of the former tram depot and the establishment of an educational programme based around food production marks the starting point of a series of thoughtful moves that generate a dialogue between existing domains and new impulses. A proposed 'Green Cross' of high-quality public spaces anchors spatially the new agglomerations on-site within the existing urban structure.

The winner project '5 Squares of Learning' goes even further and reinterprets the project site as an essential segment of a newly articulated 'Green Ring'

KLAGENFURT

interlocking with the historical ring and supporting the existing green spaces around the centre. This new green infrastructure is integrated into the spatial organisation of the site through clearly defined types of open spaces: a green boulevard, a series of small parks, and tree-lined squares. This enfilade of public spaces connects the four specific plots of the project site and links naturally with the adjacent neighbourhoods. Within the four plots, each intervention is based on the existing as a precious resource and strengthens the particular identities. Old and new structures on site are conceived as complementary and arranged in generous spatial constellations that also integrate the neighbouring areas outside the project site. Like the reused structures of the garage and the former tram depot, the proposed structures and typologies anticipate a high degree of flexibility. They are suitable for different programmes and open to change of use over extended time frames.

What remains is the question of where all the buses will move in the near future? What we once called periphery is no longer peripheral. There is almost no 'outside the city' anymore to easily outsource essential urban machinery and it is not just an ambitious strategic decision where to re-locate these elements of public infrastructure. Furthermore, it is essential to recognise them as important urban projects and to relate them to their new context in a way that they secure opportunities to build on for the future. Perhaps they could again become structural backgrounds and agents of change for our altering living cities. And what this could look like, might be a good question for an upcoming EUROPAN competition.

Benni Eder was a member of the international jury for EUROPAN 16. He is an architect in Vienna and winner of the EUROPAN 9 and EUROPAN 13 competition for sites in Austria.

INTERVIEW WITH THE SITE PARTNER

What are the main questions posed to the competitors concerning the transformation of the site?
Robert Piechl: The EUROPAN 16 site is one of the most attractive areas for urban development in the city within the next ten years. We think that in the current (global and climatic) situation the use of this land is crucially important – its location alone bears an enormous potential to provide answers for future living scenarios. Next to a regional mobility hub with a high-speed European train connection in lieu, we expect visionary ideas on living concepts without cars but with maximum mobility. Secondly, the site is located in the midst of educational institutions and, if not fenced off like it is now, would be heavily frequented by young people and those involved in education. Making use of this circumstance, we are expecting a porous, open, and inspiring quarter for learning, discovering, and exchange. Another inert characteristic is the substantial size of the site. We managed to bring together four sites, adding up to 6.1 hectares in total and thus providing a scale where concepts can enfold and make an actual impact. From the competitors, we were expecting nothing less than a pilot proposal to be imitated by others (following developments) in the future.

How is the site linked to the two subtopics of 'metabolism' and 'inclusivity'?
The term 'new learning', as described in the brief, is understood as an inclusive way of sharing knowledge: primary/secondary education meets pioneers, meets science, meets professionals, meets craftsmanship, meets innovation, meets digitisation, meets creativity, meets possibilities – for everyone. Education needs to be rethought to render a fruitful, benevolent, and exciting exploration of knowledge. This place is intended to become a lab for the cross-fertilisation of ideas, combined with social functions and workplaces on the ground floor and housing above. A range of typologies provides living spaces for people who value a centralised and well-connected location. We expect the high-speed train connection to feed into this scenario to

contribute to a mixed place, as well as the slow mobility aspect prioritising pedestrians and bikes to contribute to an engaged and lively community.

Have you already defined a specific process for the territorial and/or urban and/or architectural development of the site after the EUROPAN competition? Do you expect a proposal from the competitors linked to what they proposed in their prize-winning projects?
We came to EUROPAN at an early stage of the planning process. This was a conscious decision, as we wanted to involve new ideas from the start and set the stage for an open approach welcoming visionary input. We have asked for an urban development plan and the awarded proposal suggests a stringent and robust structure of urban sequences, which we think is very suitable. Realistically, it will take a couple of years until existing tenants move out and the first plots become available to build. Our aim is to involve and consult the winning team where possible in the further processes. Overall, we are optimistic that key ideas will remain recognisable in the finished project.

Robert Piechl is a EUROPAN 16 site representative for the City of Klagenfurt. He is the director of the Planning Department in Klagenfurt.

Bus depot with forecourt and neighbouring plot at the back, showing a private house, the Volxhalle and an office building

KLAGENFURT WINNER

5 SQUARES OF NEW LEARNING

Our site becomes an alternative, new centre of Klagenfurt – one that attracts citizens, students, and businesses. The system of existing green spaces around the historical centre is supported by a new green ring. The spine of public spaces offers a new pedestrian connection. The enfilade of public squares creates the main circulation route and forms a spine of public spaces of the site. Each of the five squares has its own scale, function, and atmosphere: Educational Square, Multipurpose Square, Makers' Square, Cultural Square, and Market Square. Each of five parks celebrates the diversity of greenery in the city. Dispersed education, as one of the main functions on the site, exists in almost every building.

PRIZE
Winner

PROJECT
5 Squares of New Learning

AUTHORS
Artem Kitaev (RU)
Architect Urbanist
Leonid Slonimskiy (RU)
Architect Urbanist
Dmitrii Prikhodko (RU)
Architect Urbanist

COLLABORATORS
Grigori Parfjonov (EE)
Urban Mobility Expert
Lavrenty Cheltsov (RU)
Student of Architecture
Diliara Nurislamova (RU)
Student of Architecture
Semen Selyutin (RU)
Student of Architecture

KOSMOS
Graz, Moscow, Zurich
k-s-m-s.com
@kosmos_architects

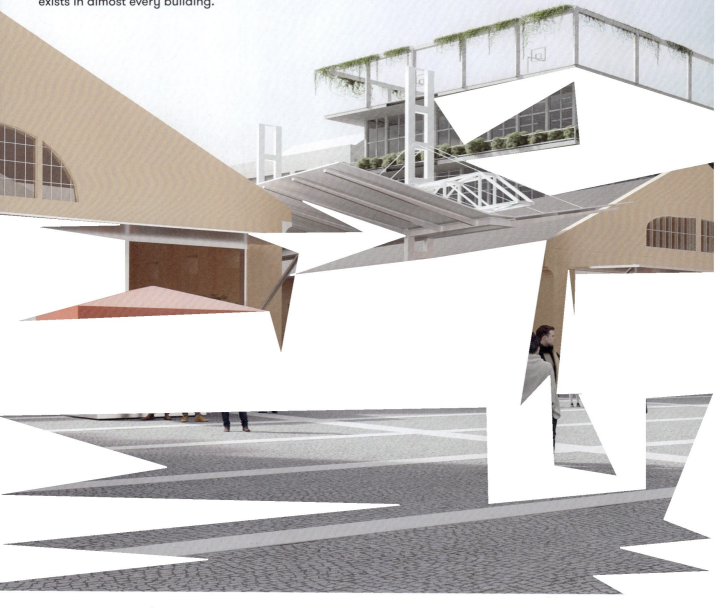

WINNER — KLAGENFURT

'The sequence of spaces conveys a certain fluidity, whereby a lot of attention is put into achieving a variety of public spaces, a sequence of squares with networked courtyards and gardens'. Jury

Visualisation showing the 'Market Square' and in due succession the 'Culture Square'

'Our project focuses not on the architecture per se, buildings, volumes, facades, but on the spaces between or around them. These spaces are created by the buildings, and normally considered as transitional, public, supplementary spaces. We believe that programming these spaces and designing their usage is one of the key roles of the contemporary architect.

Klagenfurt is a site of intriguing complexity and at the same time unusual character. It is woven from several parts that are completely different in their nature and which have very different contexts. Our project connects and interweaves it, additionally creating green and circulation rings.

It was important for us to answer the specific problems of the site through a series of simple and straightforward strategies such as regimes of use, hardware/software, and other concepts that we have developed. E16 became an experimental platform for us where we could test our ideas using the complexity of the design area and its challenges'.

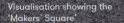

Visualisation showing the 'Makers' Square'

KLAGENFURT   WINNER   78

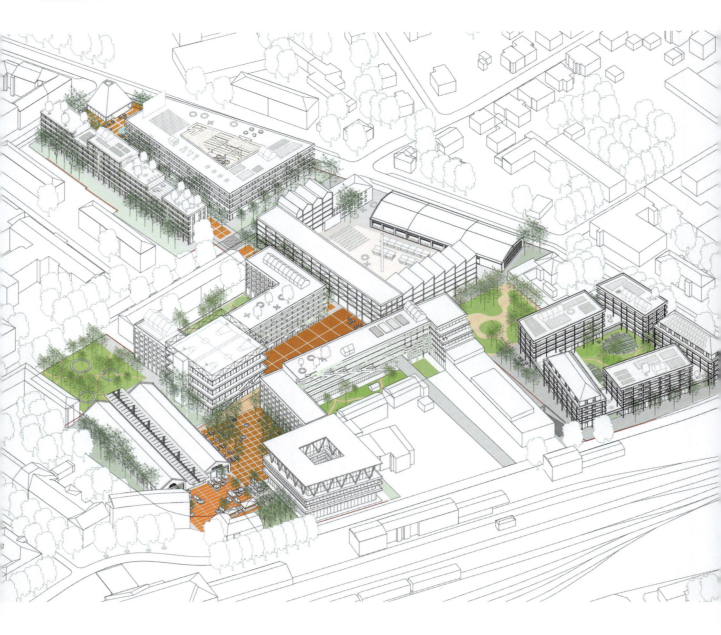

JURY STATEMENT

The jury values the strong concept, its clear presentation, and attractive narrative. The coherence between the development of the ground floors, the built volumes, and the different types of spaces is convincing, resulting in a specified urban pattern adequate for this site. The sequence of spaces conveys a certain fluidity, whereby a lot of attention is put into achieving a variety of public spaces, a sequence of squares with networked courtyards and gardens. In this respect, the programmatic labelling of the single open spaces is discussed, raising the question of 'overprogramming' and thus eventually narrowing the performative flexibility of the public spaces. Independent from the programming, the sizes and dimensions of the open spaces seem suitable to the jury and create a resilient framework for the future design. In this context, the jury suggests specifying the design of the central square with regards to climatic requirements (heat island effect in summer).

The built volumes convince through their stacked structures and their coherent width, providing a flexible system in which housing and other programmes can be accommodated responsively.

The project's careful dealing with the notion of inside-out (in-between spaces, boulevards, squares, and courtyards) is seen as a means to foster a dialogue within the site, as well as with the neighbouring areas. The prominent corridor from Südbahngürtel towards the north is questioned in its necessity and purpose.

All in all, it is much appreciated that the proposal emerges from an analysis of the larger context and incorporates the scale and tonality of the existing city.

WINNER **KLAGENFURT**

Left:
Axonometric view of the new city quarter

Above:
Ground floor plan showing the sequence of public squares and green areas with the passages connecting them all

KLAGENFURT RUNNER-UP

TRACING DOMAINS

At the heart of Viktringer Vorstadt lies a site in desperate need of structure, a resilient framework for future growth. Conditions uncovered at this location become an outset for revitalisation. They are intensified, which allow them to propagate towards one another. A properly defined network of open interiors originates where they overlap. This found urban fabric, embedded within the site, mediates the various domains at interplay, establishing a new realm for sharing, exchange, and learning. Each domain mediates with its context; combined they form a catalogue of assorted urban typologies. The site will be a laboratory for domestic prototypes mixed with interdisciplinary education and diverse green public spaces, advancing Klagenfurt as a destination along the Baltic-Adriatic corridor.

'The topic of the Klagenfurt brief fits perfectly into our previous fascinations and expertise, whilst also posing a new challenge in a new context. We approached the design task as both urban and architectural, tracing relations between the city and typologies for proposed buildings and public spaces. We like the fact that there is a beautiful ambiguity to the project. Even if it does propose to radically restructure the area, it tries to do so by taking a very sensitive approach to its context, attempting to rebuild it from the qualities and identity that can be locally uncovered today'.

PRIZE
Runner-Up

PROJECT
Tracing Domains

AUTHORS
Izabela Słodka (PL)
Architect
Xander van Dijk (NL)
Architect

Studio Iza Słodka
Rotterdam
izaslodka.com
@studio.izaslodka

Xander van Dijk architectuur
Amsterdam
xvandijk.nl

Visualisation looking east, showing the 'Crafts Passage' with the Vegetable Garden Greenhouse and Outdoor School on the right and the Bakery on the left

KLAGENFURT RUNNER-UP 82

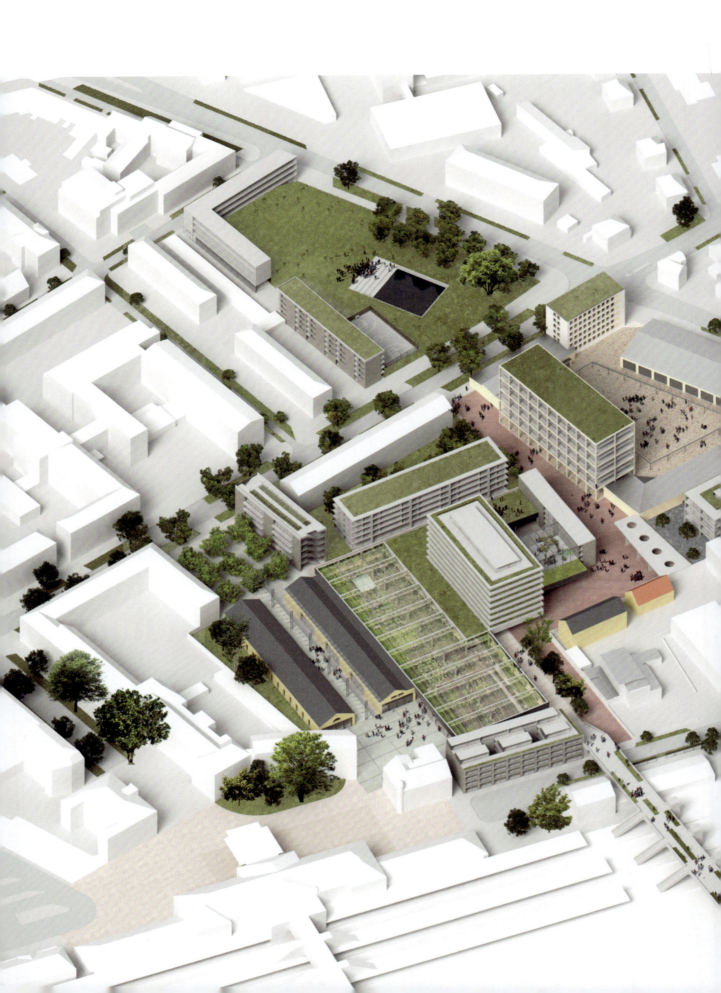

JURY STATEMENT

'Tracing Domains' is characterised by the fact that it was developed from the existing situation. The project is credited with responding specifically to the situation, on the one hand, and intensifying and strengthening what has been found, on the other. The concept proposes nine development themes and the completion of the project perimeter.

The project is valued for its comprehensively worked out structure of public spaces and for creating thoughtful continuities. It proposes a flexible logic of agglomeration of the different significant parts for which the structure of public spaces creates a unifying framework; within this framework each operation can articulate its own autonomy and its own meaning. Some jury members see a weakness in the agglomeration because it doesn't produce a new coherent structure, whilst others understand the proposal as an attractive interplay between proactive entities creating a dialogue among themselves and its in-between spaces. Such are found, for example, in the cross-programming of the micro-production of gardening, food court, kitchen, school and harvest.

The quality of walking through the public space is generally estimated highly, its elegantly meandering situation reasonably addressed: courtyards, a linear structure, covered areas... It is one of the projects that communicates with the outside in an interesting and subtle way. The strong action of the new bridge does not seem to match the overall sensitivity and is critically questioned.

'It proposes a flexible logic of agglomeration of the different significant parts for which the structure of public spaces creates a unifying framework'. Jury

KLAGENFURT RUNNER-UP

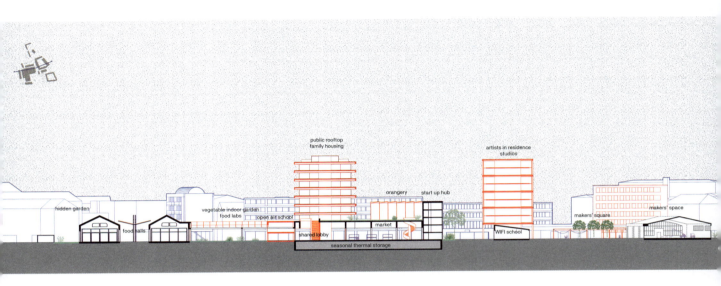

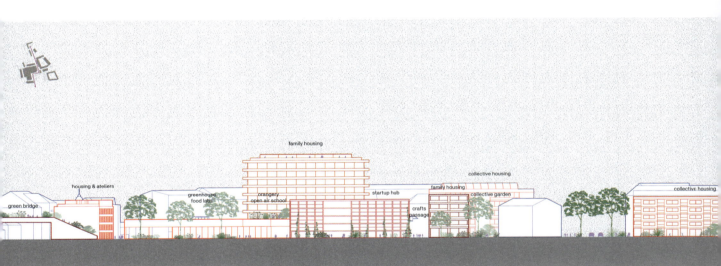

Above:
Cross-sections

Right:
Floor plan. The crucial aspect of the project site is its porosity. Public spaces float freely, changing their sizes and character, inviting inhabitants and visitors to explore diverse connections, squares, passages, and alleys in between various programmes, to interact and learn from each other.

RUNNER-UP **KLAGENFURT**

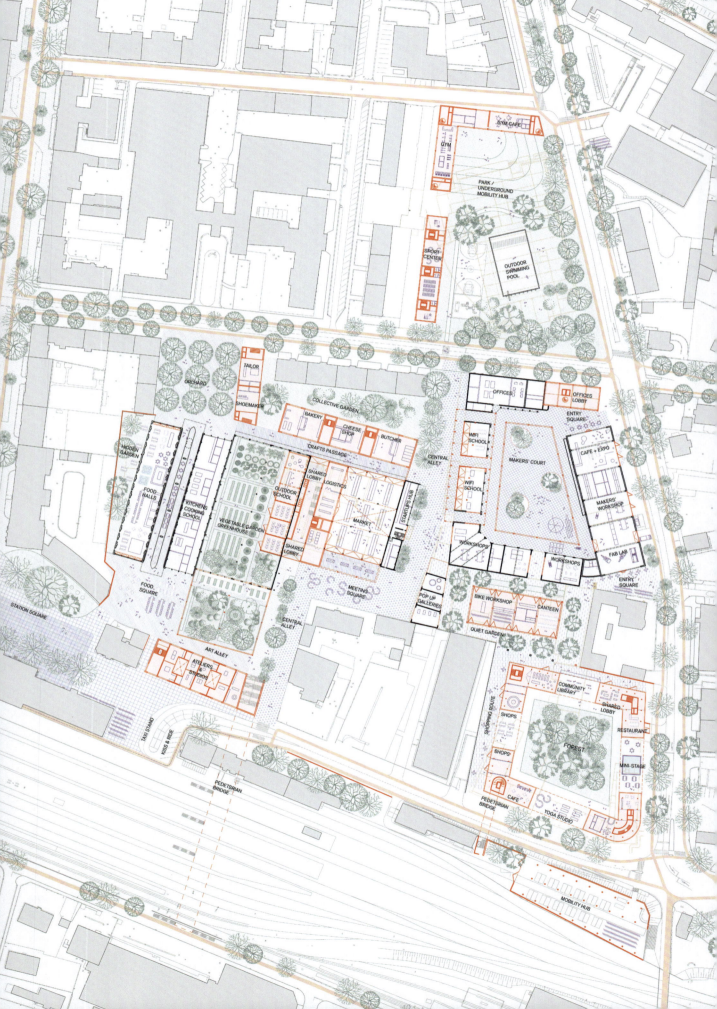

ENTRIES IN/OUT

THE WINNING TEAMS ARE BASED IN
17 DIFFERENT COUNTRIES.
55% (70 TEAMS) WON IN THEIR
COUNTRY OF RESIDENCE,
45% (57 TEAMS) WON ABROAD.

60/40% AUSTRIA

50/50% BELGIUM

82/18% FRANCE

73/27% GERMANY

20/80% ITALY

94/6% NORWAY

56/44% SPAIN

75/25% SWEDEN

71/29% SWITZERLAND

EXPANSION FROM WITHIN

LINZ

SCALE
L & XS urban and architectural prototypes

LOCATION
Linz, Austria

POPULATION
203,000 inhabitants

STUDY SITE
19.2 ha

PROJECT SITE
4 prototypes

ACTORS
EBS, City of Linz, ÖBB Austrian Federal Railways

— strategic site
⊏⊐ project site

Known today for education and culture, Linz is a regional capital on the Danube River. Historically, Linz was an important industrial city, mainly due to its steel production. During the Second World War, arms were produced on a large scale, employing a lot of people. Housing construction boomed, with the garden city concept serving as a role model used paradigmatically throughout the city for entire quarters. The E16 site derives from that era, displaying a coherent ensemble within a lush green setting; its buildings mainly date back to 1938, mixed in with some later additions with higher density. The area is characterised by its proximity to the centre and the main station but also by its above-average proportion of green space and its geological elevation, which offers a view over the city. These features make it one of Linz's most sought-after residential districts. It is an idyllic place to live, but the buildings' floor plans are outdated, and parking extensively consumes public space. The city is interested in a moderate densification, thereby enhancing connections to its wider surroundings and strengthening the nearby green network for pedestrians and bikes whilst addressing concepts to foster mobility change.

The amenities of living in and within nature are primarily associated with decentralised locations on the outskirts of the city with massive urban sprawl and sealing of the non-renewable resource of soil. The E16 site 'Froschberg' in Linz, in contrast, combines scattered living in green surroundings in a central location at affordable prices. In order to preserve this rare combination of urban qualities, it is necessary to transform the settlement into a contemporary living environment by means of sensitive urban planning and prototypical architectural interventions. As a producer of cold air for itself and the adjacent areas, the settlement is considered of high climatic value, which must be taken into account in further development measures. The city has an

LINZ

interest in an appropriate and moderate redensification to improve the connection to the settlement's wider surroundings, to link the existing green spaces, and to strengthen slow mobility concepts, as well as sustainable energy supply measures. On the individual objects, questions of public space configurations, programmatic flexibility, and microclimates are to be negotiated.

The perception of the settlement is currently dominated by cars parked in the street, which take up a large part of the public space. How could this common space in the future be given back (in some parts) to the residents of Froschberg and which new and sustainable mobility concepts can contribute to further improving the residents' mobility whilst simultaneously reducing their ecological footprint and increasing the overall qualities of shared public spaces? The settlement's central location favours the possibilities of striving for a mobility change, improving the connection to the urban fabric and at the same time generating additional value for the public space, as well as for its users.

Today, the neighbourhood's focus is largely on residential use. Whilst this focus should exist in the future, we have to ask ourselves how the coming cohabitation of different generations of residents and users can ultimately be shaped to ensure a sustainable and caring coexistence, regardless of their social status and economic background. How can a mono-functional residential area be transformed into a multi-faceted environment? How will changes in the work environment, such as increasingly working from home and more flexible schedules, affect the configuration of floor plans? How can everyday culture expand and interconnect beyond its usual means? How can the interweaving of different requirements for use and rhythms be spatially formulated into a thoughtful coexistence? Which particular functions enable exchange and encounters and how should (in particular) the ground floor areas be formulated in order to generate an overarching synergy and thus promote a lively community?

The neighbourhood should by no means be regarded as a tabula rasa – on the contrary, the existing settlement structure of Froschberg provides great potential to be constantly reflected in the planning process. The intervention here is a regenerative planning approach that recognises existing resources, such as the scattered building structure or the high proportion of green spaces, reformulates them sensitively and unfolds their inherent qualities in a contemporary manner. The potential of the topography and surrounding nature serves as a canvas for the renegotiation of density with spatial quality. Weaving the notion of sharing, layering, and co-existing into a new spatial understanding, an inclusive environment could be generated.

Froschberg's typical housing typologies within a generous green setting

Top:
Two-storey buildings housing four apartments in total, á 60 m²

Right:
Three-storey building with a developed attic and a total of 21 apartments (70 m² & 45 m²)

LINZ

PROTOTYPES THAT TELL A STORY

LINZ

Susanne Eliasson

The Froschberg housing district was built between 1938 and 1941 on the outskirts of Linz, a part of the more than 10,000 apartments constructed between 1930 and 1945 to respond to the demographic boom the city was experiencing at that time. The neighbourhood is composed of several low-density, low-rise housing typologies, ranging from the detached house to terraced apartments set in large, green, open spaces. It is representative of an urbanism relating to the garden city movement that can be found in many other cities in Europe. Standing eighty years, the buildings have proven to be a successful living environment.

The title of the competition, 'Expansion from Within' clearly states the objective for Froschberg: transforming the neighbourhood from within the housing itself. The brief asks for a prototypical approach, identifying four typologies of buildings for which prototypes of transformation should be proposed. This certainly contributes to the fact that many proposals develop similar strategies at the scale of the neighbourhood. One has to look at the proposals in detail to understand the new living qualities, often very precise ones, which are offered.

But beyond the specific idea of an architectural device for extension, the notion of 'prototype' raises several issues.

1. First, there is the idea of replicability of the system and the underlying question of specific versus generic. In what way can the proposals for Froschberg also serve as a larger reflexion?
2. Then there is the question of density. With a model of expansion from within, how much expansion is actually possible without altering the existing qualities of the neighbourhood? What is the tipping point where the density becomes a problem rather than a solution?
3. In terms of housing typologies, the prototypes explore the notion of extension for whom and for what?
Different proposals have been developed in the competition: extensions of the buildings that enlarge the existing apartments, extensions next to the buildings with new apartments, more hybrid forms of extensions...
4. Finally, the prototype raises the question of the value of the buildings and neighbourhood in terms of heritage. What is interesting in the scale of the buildings? In what way do their facades contribute to the public environment? Here, the different proposals clearly prove the malleability of the existing structures but speak quite little about their inherent qualities.

The winning proposal, 'Bio-based Idiolect', develops a strategy that implicitly touches on all four of these topics. As asked in the brief, it details prototypical interventions on four different, existing housing typologies: single-family house (type D), semi-detached housing (types B and C) and terraced housing (type A). But unlike other proposals that focus solely on the typological quality of the buildings, the prototypes articulate the existing building and its surrounding with great delicacy. The titles of each intervention are evocative of this open approach: 'touching the green', 'recovering the views', 'reaching for the sun', 'reclaiming the centre'. They refer to the prototype not solely as an architectural device, but also as an attitude towards the outside and the environment.

LINZ

The prototype for 'reclaiming the centre' applied on type A buildings is partic-ularly interesting. It proposes a densification by adding a second building delicately connected to the existing one: the existing building envelope is maintained and only slightly altered whilst the second layer proposes a more open structure that detaches itself from both the building and the ground. The plans show how the space becomes a new living area for the existing units, with the living rooms converted into new bedrooms, but with the double access that is created the space could as well become a working area for the apartments or something completely different. It opens up new possibilities whilst keeping the qualities of the existing.

The prototypes of 'Bio-based Idiolect' are a perfect example of both a specific and generic approach that is much needed when seeking to retrofit these types of neighbourhoods.

By orienting the brief towards a focus on the built environment and the possi-bilities of transformation from the point of view of housing, the discussion on the qualities of Froschberg as a collective neighbourhood and the future direction that it should take has been somewhat avoided.

The economy of maintenance over time, and the renovation of the existing structures certainly lie in the potential of new square metres, but the notion of retrofitting could also be explored through other types of interventions, such as the diversification of programmes and new types of ground management. The strategic discussion on the future of neighbourhoods such as Froschberg, on what elements in their DNA that we collectively want to maintain, still needs to be held. More than a project, the strategies of interventions that the team behind 'Bio-based Idiolect' propose will be an important contribution to this discussion, serving as a tool to collectively decide a common future.

Susanne Eliasson was a member of the international jury for EUROPAN 16. A Swedish-French architect, she is the co-founder and partner of GRAU studio.

INTERVIEW WITH THE SITE PARTNER

What are the main questions posed to the competitors concerning the transformation of the site?
Manuel Gattermayr: The most important question was how to modernise the quarter carefully without removing the qualities such as the green areas or the quiet neighbourhood. We asked them how they will modernise the existing buildings, make them barrier-free, increase the number of private and common gardens, and improve the qualities of open spaces. We also asked them how they will increase the floor space in total and for locations for new buildings.

How is the site linked to the two subtopics of 'metabolism' and 'inclusivity'?
Each part of the city plays an important role in the connection to other districts on various levels, such as logistics, social aspects, the ecology, etc. I believe successful developments are only possible if those connections are understood. Froschberg has many critical functions that are important for Linz and its citizens: It is a green oasis, it is a home for many residents, it has a very central location, and it is a well-known part of Linz's history. And it has a tremendous potential for development. This potential should be used – for current as well as future residents. Inclusivity is a very interesting characteristic in regard to Froschberg, as it is often described as a village inside the city whose residents know each other very well. On the one hand, this inclusivity of the neighbourhood is a strength of the quarter; on the other hand, it reveals the question of how to open this community to new residents.

Have you already defined a specific process for the territorial and/or urban and/or architectural development of the site after the EUROPAN competition? Do you expect a proposal from the competitors linked to what they proposed in their prize-winning projects?
We do not expect a direct translation of the proposals from the competitors. As regards implementation, it is very important that all the stakeholders are involved. In our

case, this means our tenants, the City of Linz and the EBS. In this spirit, we are interested in involving EUROPAN in a strategic process for the development of Froschberg which will lead to a specific implementation approach.

Manuel Gattermayr is a EUROPAN 16 site representative for the site in Linz. He is a project manager at EBS, where he is responsible for the revitalisation of the Froschberg area.

LINZ WINNER 98

BIO-BASED IDIOLECT

'Bio-based Idiolect' ambitiously tackles all the challenges in this special location and suggests a moderate densification where living, working, and sharing overlap in a variety of offered units. With collaboration, flexibility, and inclusivity as key qualities, the private, public, and in-between spaces are consciously re-evaluated and designed to enhance spatial experience with a full spectrum of social ambiences. By enriching the layouts, four replicable prototypes of a distinct and inviting architectural language gracefully bridge the old with the new and are supported further by a permeable, slow mobility network in the accessible, extensive green. Bio-based materials and a comprehensive sustainability and circularity strategy strengthen a vibrant, revitalised neighbourhood for decades to come.

'EUROPAN 16 marks the closing of a personal ten-year cycle dedicated to international architecture competitions. What a fine way to 'end' this trajectory (#almost40) of five consecutive EUROPAN sessions, among many other competitions. This win is of particular importance: architecturally, professionally, and symbolically. After all this time, the core values still remain the same: to be active in competitions without borders, explore the creative freedom, develop and be inspired, and hopefully bring a strong vision to the table that will fuel fruitful and lasting collaborations! Let the next cycle begin!'

PRIZE
Winner

PROJECT
Bio-based Idiolect

AUTHORS
Michalis Ntourakos (GR)
Architect/Engineer

Michalis Ntourakos
resilient.intuitive.arch¹tecture
Rotterdam
ntourakos.com
@michalis_ntourakos

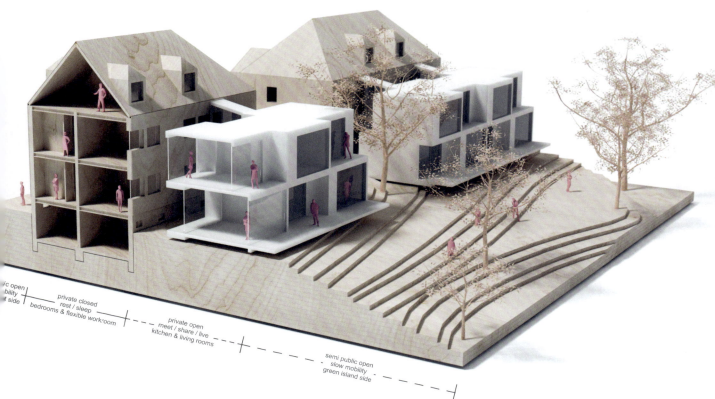

Top:
Type C 'Touching the Green'
For this garden city 'mansion', the more personal spaces occupy the existing volume and with minimal interventions ensure an extra room that can be used as a work room. The replicable 'bio-based' attachment serves as an open and light two-level shared space which secures an additional entrance and direct access to the garden for every unit.

Bottom:
Type A 'Reclaiming the Centre'
The private spaces of a flat are being located in the existing volumes, where only minimal interventions are needed. The replicable 'bio-based' extension houses the shared private spaces and secures an additional entrance with an elevator. Further flexible shared functions are located on the top and ground floor. All have direct access to the central green space.

JURY STATEMENT

The design rejects the demolition of buildings and aims to rather extend the life of the existing ones. The 'bio-based' materials used for the temporary annexes are to be returned to the material cycle and re-used at the end of the buildings' life (after 50+ years). The standardisation and the possibility to dismantle the prefabricated wooden modules should make this possible.

The project offers two different strategies of extension, either add-on with distance or add-on directly. This develops into a kind of toolbox that generates different types for different situations. The jury particularly appreciates the proposed approach for Types A and C, which formulates the idea of an additional layer positioned at a certain distance from the existing building and hardly changing it. Typologically, the project creates a kind of 'micro-courtyard' between the existing building and the new one, with the more private spaces to be housed in the existing part. The more public uses, such as living room and kitchen, are placed in the new layer with large openings facing the greenery. The jury unanimously finds this a convincing solution.

Types B and D are also modified by an additional layer, but this time it is attached directly to the existing front. This is seen sceptically because of the resulting building depth. Furthermore, additional floors are proposed here, which requires careful consideration as for possible structural constraints of the old buildings.

All interventions are planned in wood and by serial production, which makes the new intervention clearly visible. Another positive feature in this context is the sensible 'landing' of these elements, which do not simply land on the ground. Instead, a platform hovering above the ground sets a subtle but clear limit to the private space, whilst at the same time preserving the existing topography. Thereby, a clear distinction between the private and the communal public green is articulated without consuming additional spaces for borders or buffer zones.

WINNER　　LINZ

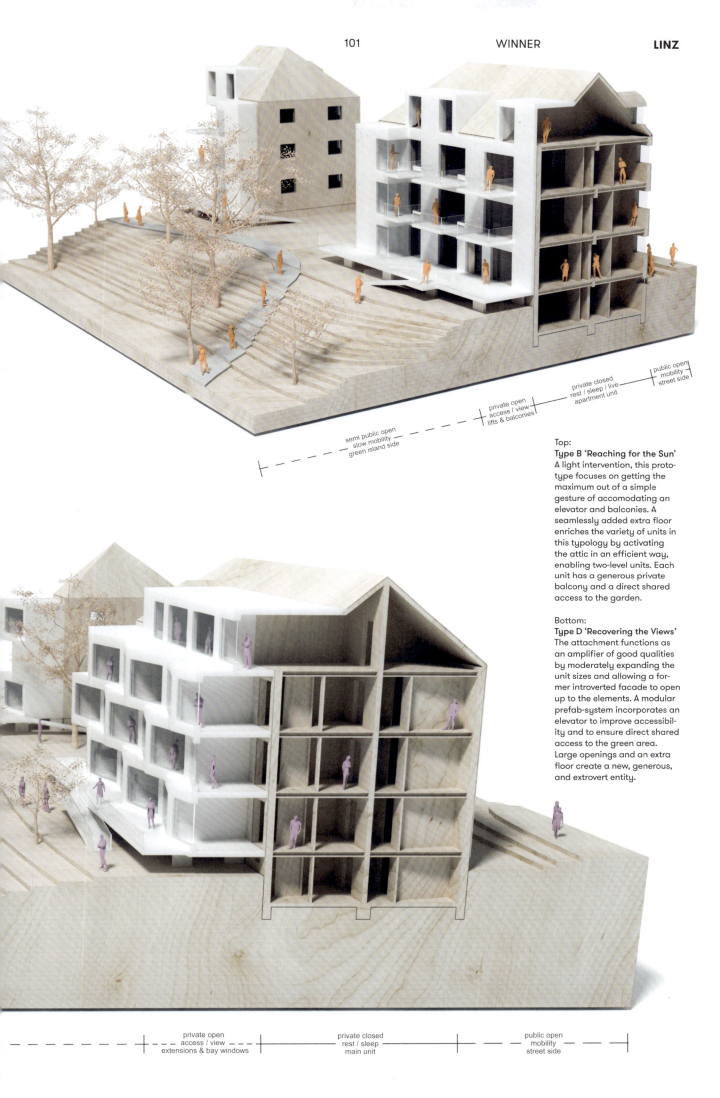

Top:
Type B 'Reaching for the Sun'
A light intervention, this prototype focuses on getting the maximum out of a simple gesture of accomodating an elevator and balconies. A seamlessly added extra floor enriches the variety of units in this typology by activating the attic in an efficient way, enabling two-level units. Each unit has a generous private balcony and a direct shared access to the garden.

Bottom:
Type D 'Recovering the Views'
The attachment functions as an amplifier of good qualities by moderately expanding the unit sizes and allowing a former introverted facade to open up to the elements. A modular prefab-system incorporates an elevator to improve accessibility and to ensure direct shared access to the green area. Large openings and an extra floor create a new, generous, and extrovert entity.

'This develops into a kind of toolbox that generates different types for different situations'. Jury

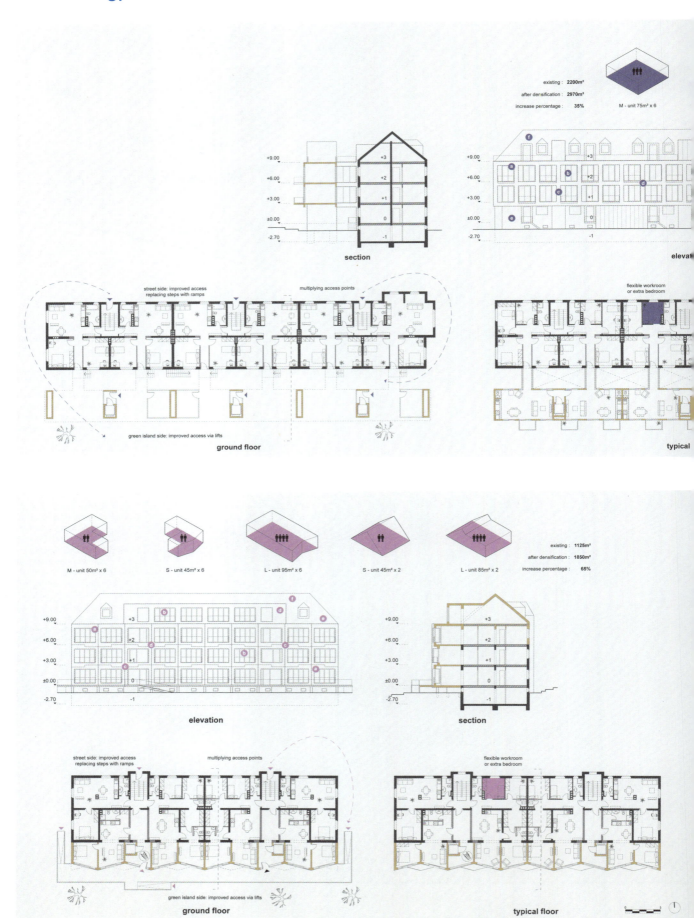

WINNER — LINZ

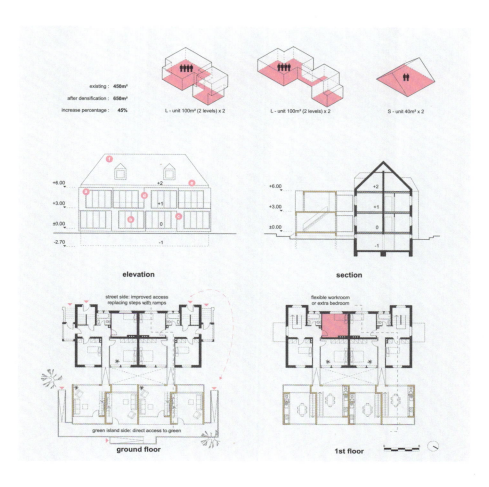
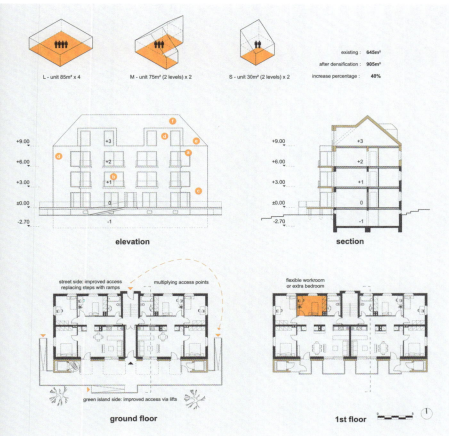

Top left:
Type A 'Reclaiming the Centre'

Top right:
Type C 'Touching the Green'

Bottom left:
Type D 'Recovering the Views'

Bottom right:
Type B 'Reaching for the Sun'

ORIGINS OF PAR- TICIPANTS

FOR THE AUSTRIAN SI

168 PARTICIPANTS IN TOTAL FROM ALL OVER THE WORLD WORKING ON THE AUSTRIAN SITES

ITALY 59

AUSTRIA 25

SPAIN 17

POLAND 11

CHINA 9
GERMANY 8
RUSSIA 7

ARGENTINA, FRANCE 5

CZECH REPUBLIC, NETHERLANDS 3
CANADA 2
ESTONIA, GREECE, INDIA, IRAN, LITHUANIA, NORTH MACEDONIA, PORTUGAL, ROMANIA, UK, USA, VENEZUELA 1

JURY PROCEDURE

To assess the work, each nation sets up an international panel of experts, which selects the prize winners in a two-stage, Europe-wide synchronised, anonymous jury procedure.

1ST STAGE: LOCAL COMMISSION
In the first stage, a local expert commission selects 30%–35% (or a minimum of five entries) of the best works. The local commission consists of: three local representatives of the city and landowners, two architects or urban planners from the local context (e.g., design advisory board), two representatives (expert jurors) of the international EUROPAN jury, and an international expert panel nominated by EUROPAN Austria.

2ND STAGE: INTERNATIONAL JURY
The international jury of EUROPAN Austria meets to nominate the winners for the Austrian locations from the anonymous pre-selection of the 30%–40% of the best projects.

The international jury has received and is aware of all projects submitted on the Austrian sites and has the right to bring a project that was not pre-selected in the first stage of evaluation back into the discussion.

LOCAL COMMISSIONS

GRAZ
Martin Poppmeier, site owner CITYPARK Graz
Wilfried Krammer, executive office for urban planning, development and construction, City of Graz
Bernhard Inninger, head of planning department, City of Graz
Aglaée Degros, architect and urban planner, professor at the Technical University Graz, head of the Institute of Urbanism
Sonja Frühwirth, architect, principal Atelier Frühwirth, Graz
Bernd Vlay, international jury member
Benni Eder, international jury member

KLAGENFURT
Robert Piechl, head of city planning, City of Klagenfurt
Georg Wald, city planning Klagenfurt
Bernhard Eder, KMG Klagenfurt Mobil GmbH
Sharing one vote:
Christiane Holzinger, federal chair of the Junior Chamber of Commerce, Carinthia and **Folker Schabkar,** CEO FSF Real Estate
Aglaée Degros, architect and urban planner, professor at the Technical University Graz, head of the Institute of Urbanism

Reinhard Hohenwarter, architect, partner at 3KANT Architekten
Bernd Vlay, international jury member
Daniela Herold, international jury member

LINZ
Gerald Aichhorn, managing director of WAG
Manuel Gattermayr, project manager for Froschberg, WAG
Gunther Kolouch, head of planning department, City of Linz
Evelyn Rudnicki, architect, partner at pool Architektur, Vienna
Gerhard Sailer, architect, partner at Halle 1 Architektur, Salzburg
Bernd Vlay, international jury member
Daniela Herold, international jury member

JURY

INTERNATIONAL JURY

SUSANNE ELIASSON (FR) 2ND CHAIR OF JURY
Susanne Eliasson is a Swedish-French architect and founding partner of GRAU (Good Reasons to Afford Urbanism). The office works in the space between architecture and urbanism, developing urban visions to transform our common environment. Through numerous urban renewal projects, strategic studies on densification, masterplan proposals for new districts and ongoing research on horizontal urbanism, the practice has developed a strong expertise on issues relating to housing. Susanne Eliasson received the 'Young Planners Award' from the French Ministry of Housing and Sustainable Habitat in 2016. She was appointed advising architect for the City of Bordeaux in 2021.

ANDREAS HOFER (CH)
Andreas Hofer was born in Lucerne. He studied architecture at the Swiss Institute for Technology in Zurich. In 2018 he was elected as director for the International Building Exhibition in Stuttgart (Internationale Bauausstellung 2027 StadtRegion Stuttgart). In Zurich he mainly worked as a consultant and project developer for innovative cooperative housing projects such as 'Kraftwerk1' and 'mehr als wohnen' (more than housing). Andreas Hofer regularly publishes in various media on architecture, urban development, and housing issues, accompanies housing projects as a jury member in competitions and is involved in teaching at universities.

ELKE KRASNY (AT)
Elke Krasny, PhD, professor of art and education and head of the Institute for Education in the Arts at the Academy of Fine Arts Vienna. Krasny's scholarship, academic writings, curatorial work, and international lectures address questions of care at the present historical conjuncture with a focus on emancipatory and transformative practices in art, curating, architecture, and urbanism. The 2019 exhibition and edited volume *Critical Care. Architecture and Urbanism for a Broken Planet*, curated and edited together with Angelika Fitz, was published by The MIT Press and introduces

a care perspective in architecture, addressing the anthropocenic conditions of the global present.

ELISABETH MERK (D)
Prof. Dr. (University of Florence) Elisabeth Merk, architect, has been the City of Munich's planning director since 2007. After freelance work and further education in Florence, she was responsible for urban design, urban monument preservation, and special projects in Munich and Regensburg from 1995 to 2000. She headed the urban development and urban planning division in Halle/Saale from 2000 to 2005. Elisabeth Merk had a regular professorship at the HFT Stuttgart from 2005–2007, has been an honorary professor there since 2009, has served as the president of the German Academy for Urban and Regional Spatial Planning (DASL) since 2015 and has been an honorary professor at the Technical University of Munich (TUM) since 2020.

AKIL SCAFE-SMITH (UK)
Akil Scafe-Smith is one sixth of RESOLVE, an interdisciplinary design collective that aims to address multi-scalar social challenges by combining architecture, art, technology, and engineering. RESOLVE have delivered numerous projects, workshops, and talks, in London, the UK, and across Europe, as well as working with a variety of initiatives and institutions to pilot projects that introduce young people from under-represented backgrounds to concepts in interdisciplinary design. RESOLVE are also currently unit leaders at the Architectural Association, research fellows at Het Nieuwe Instituut in Rotterdam, and resident creative youth workers at the V&A East/VARI in London.

PAOLA VIGANÒ (IT)
Paola Viganò is an architect and urbanist. She is a professor of urban theory and urban design at the EPFL (Lausanne), where she heads the Lab-U and the new interdisciplinary Habitat Research Centre. She is also a professor at IUAV University Venice and a guest professor at several international schools. She received the title Doctor Honoris Causa UCL in 2016, the Grand Prix de

JURY

From left:
Elisabeth Merk, Benni Eder, Andreas Hofer, Susanne Eliasson, Akil Scafe-Smith, Bernd Vlay, Paola Viganò

l'Urbanisme in 2013, the Flemish Culture Award for Architecture in 2017, and the Golden Medal Career Award of the Milano Triennale in 2018. She founded Studio Associato with Bernardo Secchi (1990–2014); since 2015 Studio Paola Viganò has been working on urban landscape projects and public spaces in Europe and has won several international competitions.

BERND VLAY (AT) CHAIR OF JURY

Bernd Vlay is an architect and urbanist based in Vienna, and together with Lina Streeruwitz he is the director of the office StudioVlayStreeruwitz. The office has been realizing large scale urban and architectural projects, combining architecture, urbanism, and research from local to translocal scales. In 2018 the office received the Hans Hollein Art Prize for Architecture, in 2019 it was shortlisted for the Mies van der Rohe prize with the project 'Performative Brise-Soleil'. Bernd Vlay pursues teaching activities at various schools and is a member of numerous advisory boards in the field of urban development, design, and architecture (Linz, Innsbruck, and BIG). He is the president of EUROPAN Austria and a member of the Scientific Committee of EUROPAN Europe.

SUBSTITUTES

BENNI EDER (AT)

Benni Eder studied architecture in Vienna and Santiago de Chile. In 2008 he co-founded studio uek prior to establishing his current practice, studio ederkrenn, with Theresa Krenn in 2017. His award-winning EUROPAN 9 project 'Oase 22' was nominated for the Mies van der Rohe Award in 2015. Benni Eder understands architecture as a collaborative cultural practice and has since been working on the conception and realisation of architecture and urban development projects of different scales. Since 2009 he has also been teaching at the Technical University in Vienna.

DANIELA HEROLD (AT)

Daniela Herold is an architect based in Linz and Vienna. She has been a senior scientist at the Institute for Art and Architecture at the Academy of Fine Arts Vienna since 2009, where she has been teaching within the platform of Geography Landscape and Cities. In parallel she runs her own practice, THuM Ateliers, together with the architect Rolf Touzimsky. The practice won the EUROPAN 7 site competition in Salzburg. Their project 'Parklife' was completed in 2012 and nominated for the Bauherrenpreis 2012. Recently, the practice was involved in drawing up a future urban development strategy for Linz, for which scenarios relating to the topic of 'Stadtleben' (City Life) have been generated.

TEAMS

GRAZ

FREE MÜHLGANG
Violeta Ordóñez Manjón (ES) Architect
Raquel Ruiz García (ES) Architect
Mónica Lamela Blázquez (ES) Architect
We met at the Architecture School of Madrid (ETSAM) and have since kept exchanging ideas. We explore and learn, through design, other ways of becoming socially helpful, enhancing participation, freedom of use, and appropriation.
Each of us has implemented projects and successfully participated in a variety of competitions within the architecture offices we have collaborated with. Our practise is enriched by other disciplines such as anthropology, gender studies, photography, ceramics, graphic design, and fashion. After years of wandering across the world, EUROPAN 16 gave us the chance to reconnect and materialise dreams, ideals, programmes, and concepts we pursue.
We are currently based in Madrid and Los Angeles.

POST-SHOPPING
Pedro Pitarch Alonso (ES) Architect
Pedro Pitarch is an architect (ETSAM) and a musician (COM, Caceres).
He is an associate teacher at ETSAM (UPM) and has been a Teaching Fellow in Architectural Design at the Bartlett School of Architecture (UCL) and Steedman Fellow at the Washington University in St Louis. His work has been exhibited at the 16th and 17th Venice Architecture Biennale, the 4th Lisbon Architecture Triennale, SBAU 2021, the Triennale Milan and the Vienna Design Week.
In 2015 he founded 'Pedro Pitarch Architectures & Urbanisms', an architectural office based in Madrid. His projects have been awarded in several international competitions. His practise focuses on the interrelations between architecture, contemporary culture production, and the construction of societies.

URBAN SOLUTIONS SUPERSTRUCTURE
Rene Dapperger (DE) Architect
During my studies at the University of Stuttgart I had already started to take part in different competitions to explore the architectural opportunities beyond the academical boundaries. Having worked in different offices during my student years, I experienced the workflow of variable urbanistic and architectural scales. It also became clear that working on projects that have an impact on everyday life was a big component for me. I also won the Schinkel Prize together with my colleague Felix Hauff one year ago, which was quite a similar experience, implementing a project in a previously unfamiliar context. After completing my Master's degree I started working at se\arch in Stuttgart, exploring new concepts for contemporary architecture.

KLAGENFURT

5 SQUARES OF NEW LEARNING
KOSMOS
Artem Kitaev (RU), Architect Urbanist
Leonid Slonimskiy (RU), Architect Urbanist
Dmitrii Prikhodko (RU), Architect Urbanist
KOSMOS architects (founded in 2014) is an award-winning architectural office which works from Zurich, Graz, and Moscow. Amongst other prizes, KOSMOS won the Prix de Genève for Experimental Architecture, got nominated for the Swiss Art and Design Awards, and received the Milano Archmarathon Award, the Pro Helvetia Prize for the Swiss Pavilion at the Prague Quadrennial, and many others. The work of KOSMOS has been widely published and exhibited, including at the Venice Biennale, the American Institute of Architects, and the Swiss Architecture Museum. KOSMOS designs and builds projects of diverse scales and types: from art installations and temporary pavilions to big public buildings such as sport centres, museums, and airports, as well as masterplans and large urban parks.

TRACING DOMAINS
Izabela Słodka (PL), Architect
Xander van Dijk (NL), Architect
Izabela Słodka is an architect based in Rotterdam (NL). After winning the EUROPAN 15 competition in 2019 with the 'Makers' Maze' project, she established her own studio (Studio Iza Słodka). Iza's main interests and experience focus on the revitalisation of post-industrial sites and designing spaces for manufacturing. She is a guest teacher at the Rotterdam Academy of Architecture. Currently living in Amsterdam, Xander van Dijk is a Dutch architect originally from Heerlen. He has held positions at a number of offices, often involved in projects for city infrastructure and urban transformation, always making sure to set aside time to pursue independent work. In recent years he has been teaching at the Technical University in Delft.

LINZ

BIO-BASED IDIOLECT
Michalis Ntourakos (GR), Architect/Engineer
Internationally oriented like the city of Rotterdam where Michalis Ntourakos is based, his studio recognises a suitable platform for innovative architecture in international competitions. Designing beyond borders opens up possibilities to experiment and reach new grounds in a variety of typologies and environments. A particular interest in mixed use projects combines with an increased focus in developing buildings out of solid wood and the integration of circular economy strategies. The practise approaches architecture as an intuitive yet scientific answer to a request concerning space. Central elements are areas of collective interest and the dynamics between public and private zones. Each design strives towards a state of 'critical happiness' which can be described as spatial well-being with a critical view.

TIMELINE

INTERSESSIONS FORUM
DIGITAL
18.01.–22.01.2021

KICK-OFF EVENT
DIGITAL
08.04.2021

SITE VISIT
GRAZ, AT
29.04.2021

TIMELINE

SITE VISIT
LINZ, AT
06.05.2021

SITE VISIT
KLAGENFURT, AT
07.05.2021

INTERNAL WORKSHOP DAY
LAKE TRAUNSEE, AT
22.07.–23.07.2021

TIMELINE

114

RESIDENCY WINWINOFFICE
CLUB HYBRID
GRAZ, AT
25.07.–30.07.2021

SECRETARIATS MEETING
SAN DONÀ, IT
05.09.–07.09.2021

LOCAL COMISSIONS
GRAZ, KLAGENFURT, LINZ, AT
11.10.–21.10.2021

FORUM OF CITIES & JURIES
SAN SEBASTIÁN, ES
04.11.–06.11.2021

INTERNATIONAL JURY
SAN SEBASTIÁN, ES
07.11.2021

CREDITS

All project images are copyrights of the teams, except stated otherwise. Project Free Mühlgang CC-BY-NC-ND

15	1. Tyranny, detail © Bas Princen, installation 14th Architecture Biennale, Venice
16	2. Tyranny, landscape © Bas Princen, installation 14th Architecture Biennale, Venice
18	3. Tyranny, gate © Bas Princen, installation 14th Architecture Biennale, Venice
21	4. Tyranny, people © Bas Princen, installation 14th Architecture Biennale, Venice
22	5. Good governance, people © Bas Princen, installation 14th Architecture Biennale, Venice
25	6. Good governance, gate © Bas Princen, installation 14th Architecture Biennale, Venice
26	7. Good governance, landscape © Bas Princen, installation 14th Architecture Biennale, Venice
29	8. Good governance, detail © Bas Princen, installation 14th Architecture Biennale, Venice
30	Ambrogio Lorenzetti, The Allegory of Good and Bad Government, Sala dei Nove, Palazzo Pubblico, Siena, 1338–1339. Source: Wikimedia Commons, Public Domain
34	Map data © OpenStreetMap contributors, SCHWARZ-PLAN.eu, figure ground plan Graz
35	Stadtvermessung Graz ©, orthophoto of site
36–37	EUROPAN Austria
38	Stadtvermessung Graz ©, aerial view
42–43	EUROPAN Austria
64	Map data © OpenStreetMap contributors, SCHWARZ-PLAN.eu, figure ground plan Klagenfurt
65	Google.at © 2021 CNES/Airbus, GeoContent, Geoimage Austria, Maxar Technologies, Kartendaten
68	EUROPAN Austria
68	Google Earth
72–73	EUROPAN Austria
88	Map data © OpenStreetMap contributors, SCHWARZ-PLAN.eu, figure ground plan Linz
89	© BEV, CC BY 4.0.
91	EUROPAN Austria
92	Stadt Linz, Pertlwieser Heimo/PTU, aerial picture
96–97	EUROPAN Austria
106	EUROPAN Austria
109	EUROPAN Austria
110	Left column, top, team picture 'Free Mühlgang', Violeta Ordóñez Manjón, Christina Ramos, Pedro Gaxiola
110	Left column, bottom, team picture 'Post-Shopping', Pedro Pitarch
110	Right column, team picture 'Urban Solutions Super-structure', Jule Büchle
111	Left column, top, team picture '5 Squares of New Learning', Rodion Kitaev
111	Left column, bottom, team picture 'Tracing Domains', Roos Pulskens
111	Right column, team picture 'Bio-based Idiolect', E. Ntourakos
112	Left column, all, EUROPAN Austria
112	Middle column, EUROPAN Austria, bottom picture, Christian Haas
112	Right column, Wilfried Krammer, except top picture, EUROPAN Austria
113	Left column, all, Manuel Gattermayr
113	Middle column, all, EUROPAN Austria
113	Right column, all, EUROPAN Austria
114	Left column, top two pictures, EUROPAN Austria, bottom two pictures, Heide Oberhuber
114	Middle column, all, EUROPAN Austria
114	Right column, all, EUROPAN Austria
115	EUROPAN Austria

Text fragments might be taken from the site briefs. With kind permission of the authors: Tobias Brown for Graz, Linda Lackner for Linz, and Iris Kaltenegger for Klagenfurt.

EUROPAN has acted as an international platform in Europe since 1989. It is one of the world's largest competitions for architects and urban designers under the age of forty and provides a forum for young professionals to develop and present their ideas for current urban challenges. For the cities and developers, EUROPAN is a tool to find innovative architectural and urban solutions for implementation. Every two years the competition is organised simultaneously and accompanied by international forums, exhibitions, and events. Around fifty European cities and over one thousand international teams participate in each session.

EUROPAN is a European federation of national structures, with Austria being one of the founding members. At the national level, EUROPAN Austria manages the jointly composed European programme and acts as a local guarantor for developing new solutions and connecting pilot projects with decision-makers.

BOARD EUROPAN AUSTRIA:
Bernd Vlay, president,
Alexandra Würz-Stalder, vice president,
**Aglaée Degros, Iris Kaltenegger,
Bart Lootsma, Claudia Nutz, Andreas Tropper, Bertram Werle**

TEAM EUROPAN AUSTRIA:
Iris Kaltenegger, secretary general,
Daniela Moosbauer, Dorothee Huber

EUROPAN Europe is based in Paris.
europan-europe.eu

EUROPAN Austria is a non-profit association, registered in Graz, registration number ZVR-690746338.

Contact:
c/o Haus der Architektur
Palais Thinnfeld,
Mariahilferstrasse 2, 8020 Graz
Maria-Lassnig-Straße 32/2,
1100 Wien
office@europan.at
www.europan.at

SITE REPRESENTATIVES:

GRAZ
City of Graz: **Wilfried Krammer**
Site owner: **Martin Poppmeier**

KLAGENFURT
City of Klagenfurt: **Robert Piechl**
KMG Klagenfurt Mobil GmbH: **Erwin Smole**
Carinthian Chamber of Commerce:
Jürgen Mandl
FSF Real Estate: **Folker Schabkar**

LINZ
WAG, EBS Wohnen Linz: **Gerald Aichhorn, Horst Irsiegler, Manuel Gattermayr**
City of Linz: **Gunther Kolouch, Christian Strecker**

We would like to thank all teams, partners, actors, and organisations for having been open to travel with EUROPAN and to enter a sphere of productive uncertainty – the only starting point for honest and responsible innovation.

IMPRINT

Editors: Iris Kaltenegger, Bart Lootsma, EUROPAN Austria
Copy editing, proofreading: Brian Dorsey
Design: sensomatic
Printing and binding: Medienfabrik Graz

© 2022 EUROPAN Austria, Graz, and Park Books AG, Zurich

© For the texts: the authors
© For the images: the architects and photographers

Park Books
Niederdorfstrasse 54
8001 Zurich, Switzerland
www.park-books.com

Park Books is being supported by the Federal Office of Culture with a general subsidy for the years 2021–2024.

All rights reserved; no part of this publication may be reproduced, stored in a retrieval system or transmitted in any form or by any means, electronic, mechanical, photocopying, recording, or otherwise, without the prior written consent of the publisher.

ISBN 978-3-03860-296-5

EUROPAN Austria is being supported by the Ministry of the Federal Republic of Austria for Arts, Culture, Civil Service and Sport.

Bundesministerium
Kunst, Kultur,
öffentlicher Dienst und Sport